ABOUT THE AUTHOR

Amitabh Bachchan was born in Allahabad on October 11, 1942 and was educated in Nainital and Delhi. After graduation he took up a job in a shipping firm in Kolkata. He took his first step into films after producer-director Khwaja Ahmed Abbas cast him in his film, *Saat Hindusthani*. In his eventful career spanning 30 odd years and over 100 films, Amitabh won several Filmfare awards and a National Award. The second phase of the Bachchan saga began with the phenomenal success of the television show *Kaun Banega Crorepati*.

A BBC survey chose him the Superstar of the Millennium over such greats as Charlie Chaplin and Laurence Olivier. He is the first Indian film star to be immortalized at Madam Tussaud's Wax Museum, London. He is the only Asian to be featured on the Wogan Show. Last year the Government of India honoured him with the Padma Bhushan for his contribution to Indian Cinema.

GW00683460

STAR PLUS™ PRESENTS

Soul Curry
for you and me

AMITABH BACHCHAN

EDITORIAL INPUT BY **R.D. TAILANG**

Published by

PopulaR
prakashan

ISBN 81–7154–984–5
(3736)

Book Design by Simrit Brar

Illustrations by Shaaz Ahmed

© 2002 Star India Private Limited

First Printed September 2002.

Enquiries regarding the sales of this book may be directed to sales@popularprakashan.com

Originally published in Hindi in January 2002 by Popular Prakashan Private Limited as *Amitabh Ka Khazana*.

Translation from Hindi by Shraddha Jahagirdar–Saxena

Processing by Supressa Graphics Pvt. Ltd.
Printed in India by Vakil & Sons Pvt. Ltd.
Industry Manor, 2nd Floor, Appasaheb Marathe Marg,
Worli, Mumbai 400 025.

Published by Ramdas Bhatkal for
Popular Prakashan Pvt. Ltd.
35–C, Pt. Madan Mohan Malaviya Marg,
Popular Press Building, Tardeo,
Mumbai 400 034

PUBLiSHER'S NOTE

Life is not always a bed of roses. Everyday, we encounter
several situations that worry us. We flip through books in order to
find quick solutions to our problems. In sheer desperation, we run
from pillar to post and seek the advice of our friends and family
members. Yet, we are not happy with the answers we get. We then
look for a guide, who will help us to tide over difficult
circumstances. A philosopher, who will reinforce our confidence
and enthusiasm, and guide us on the road towards success.

This book embodies Amitabh Bachchan's philosophy. You can
say it contains the essence of his manifold experiences. The man
needs no introduction. He is one of those extraordinary men who
have reached the very pinnacle of success. Like his life, this book
too contains simple homilies that will help you forge ahead.
Amitabh Bachchan's thought process, his personality, has
influenced and is reflected in the choice of subjects and the
phraseology of this book. Every word has his characteristic
confidence and zest for life. Amitabh speaks holistically when he
talks about every individual being complete in himself or herself.

You will definitely stop and ponder over what he says. For
instance, he remarks that honesty is the best policy, yet a lie told
for the sake of others is not evil. Two seemingly contradictory
statements co-exist in his frame of values. Think about what he
says and you are bound to agree! You will experience similar
feelings while reflecting on his remarks about words, time, culture,
learning, health, life and a host of other topics intimately connected
with our lives. In his homilies he often refers to ancient texts and

scriptures, incidents and folk tales. He inspires you and simultaneously imparts valuable lessons.

His inspiration spurs you to move ahead. Take a look at what he says about the ideal gift. For an enemy it would be forgiveness, for a friend a place in your heart, for your opponents acceptance, for your children appropriate advice, for your father respect and for your mother, the best possible gift would be your achievements. And for yourself? Nothing could be better than nurturing your abilities and converting your failures into successes. He looks upon initiative as the first and most important step towards reaching your goal. And considers failure as a mere step in the ladder to progress.

He often draws on his experience. He knows from personal experience that an idea is extremely short-lived. Hence it is best to take action as soon as it blossoms. Otherwise you might just lose it or it may fade away into oblivion. Hence he emphasises that not only must you implement your ideas but also ensure that your thought process remains alive and evergreen.

He has presented a simple and effective point of view on a variety of topics. He emphasises the similarities and differences in many things. Like good and bad children, contentment, the past-present and future, husband-wife, loss-victory, pride and respect, good and evil, to practise and to merely preach, the extraordinary and the ordinary, etc. His advice is so easy to follow that it automatically imparts learning and wisdom. After reading what he has said, you come away a more complete individual.

He examines sayings that have been passed on from

generation to generation. "From dust thou art and to dust thou shalt return." Amitabh gives this age-old truth an unusual interpretation. The saying underlines the fact that man is born empty-handed and departs from this world... also empty-handed.

But he points out that this is an illusion. As a newborn baby, a man brings with him, in his tightly closed fists, a lot of hopes and potentialities. He brings happiness for those who are close to him. And when he leaves the world, he is not empty-handed, says Amitabh. He takes with him the credit for all his achievements, the love of his people and the respect and blessings he has garnered in his life.

Or take a look at what he says here:

Once upon a time a painter made a portrait of Time. He created a beautiful, smiling portrait that was standing with both its hands stretched out. Its thick hair flopped on its forehead, but the back of its head was completely bald. The artiste maintained, "When the time is right, it beckons you to seize the moment. Hence its arms are outstretched. If you grab it by the hair in front, you will be able to control it. If, however you let the moment pass by, then your hands will only find its bald head. And then time will be out of your control." Hence Amitabh urges you to seize the moment. For you live only once and opportunity also knocks at your door... only once!

We would like to point out that this book is unique. It contains the invaluable advice and thoughts of the man of the millennium – Amitabh Bachchan!

PREFACE

It is extremely difficult to write a preface to any book. When the time came to write the preface to this book, I first thought of friends who could have helped me in writing it.

But the language of my friends was theirs, not mine. I wasn't satisfied. I thought I would draw a leaf from my father's book. But once again, it was his language not mine.

What I have written in this book is entirely my own handiwork. I have expressed my own views, thoughts and opinions. I have penned it myself. It may be right or wrong, complicated or simple. But it is mine. I am happy.

When we were doing the initial spadework to telecast *Kaun Banega Crorepati*, we toyed with different ideas of how to take it to the audiences. One idea emerged: At the beginning of every episode we thought of presenting little nuggets of knowledge and wisdom. I know that this is not a new practice. It is an old tradition in our Indian culture. What I am presenting now is a compilation of all those utterances. The thoughts are mine. But, to help me bring them to fruition, I have received invaluable contributions from Mrs. Pushpa Bharati, wife of the late litterateur Dr. Dharamveer Bharati. Writer R.D. Tailang of STAR TV and his team too were of immense help. Without their inputs, perhaps these words of wisdom would not have crystallized and reached you.

It is a matter of great pride to me that what was said on *Kaun Banega Crorepati* is now being presented to you in the form of a book. Whatever I have achieved in life is due first to God, and then to my parents. It is a result of my upbringing. My mother's love and affection is reflected in my achievements. What I have done also embodies the essence of my father's art and knowledge. I am very fortunate to have such parents. I dedicate this book to both of them!

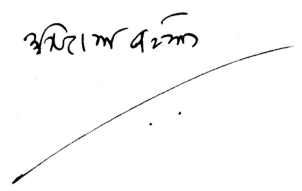

I dedicate this book to Ma and Babuji

TABLE OF CONTENTS

Soul Curry
for you and me

Recognising Wisdom

1

It is not necessary to go to a teacher, an expert or a celebrity to acquire profound knowledge. It is not mandatory either that good things of life be found in good places only. There is a saying which encapsulate this fact pithily. It goes something like this:

Gain knowledge from persons, however dull and thick
Gold is never spurned even when found in muck.

When you spot pearls of wisdom do not hesitate to pick them up. It does not matter even if they come from an unintelligent person.

> **What is intrinsically good will never change its character, no matter where it is found.**

One does not leave gold untouched, when one discovers the yellow metal in filth. One is ever ready to pick it up. What is intrinsically good will never change its character, no matter where it is found. A diamond is often spotted amidst black blocks of coal. Lotus blossoms in a swamp and the beautiful rose blooms among thorns. In fact, the

presence of such invaluable wonders enhances the importance of a place no matter how sullied it is!

Paradoxes

2

The vast world that we have inherited is full of contrasts. People are different and things differ too. There are as many perspectives as there are people. Nature herself exhibits and stamps its conformity on this diversity.

> *Let there be differences in the outer world but our mind should be free of paradoxes.*

Yet many things, though ostensibly dissimilar, share the same characteristics. What is common in a flower without fragrance and a paper bloom? Both lack fragrance. How different is a parched river from an arid desert? Both fail to quench thirst. Is a treacherous friend different from a sworn enemy? Both are equally dangerous. Is a caustic remark any different from a sharp dart? Both hold the power to wound deeply. Like a coward a timid person too is scared to confront the challenges of life.

Let there be differences in the outer world but our mind should be free of paradoxes.

Soul Curry
for you and me

Every individual is Complete in Himself

Every individual whether noble or ignoble, strong or weak, learned or uneducated, physically fit or disabled holds within him or her, the seeds of greatness.

Let the sceptics seek other gods,
We proclaim that man is the lord of the universe.

The famous American author Dale Carnegie says: You should dream of becoming as mighty as a mountain peak.

> **Status does not determine our success or failure. Our merit is assessed only on the basis of our capabilities.**

If you cannot, then aspire to be the pine tree that grows on it. If you do not succeed, be a small, beautiful tree that grows in a valley or beside a spring. If you do not achieve this, yearn to be a bush. If not a bush, try and be the soft grass that carpets the rough roads and makes pleasant the journey of a weary traveller. And, if you cannot be even this, then strive to be at least a narrow path!

Remember that status does not determine our success or failure. Our merit is assessed only on the basis of our capabilities.

We do not really have to imitate others. We must remain true to ourselves and achieve what we are capable of. And we can in this manner become truly great!

Better Virtues

It is good to praise others but it is important to look for faults within oneself. It is nice to be concerned about people but to be introspective is even nicer.

I do not deny the importance of truthfulness, but sometimes an untruth, which benefits someone, may turn out to be a better alternative. It is important to have an impeccable character but it is more important to spread love and compassion.

> **Believe in your own strengths but have faith in others' capabilities.**

To win in sports is exciting, but to lose your heart in love is exhilarating. Repay debts, perform your duty and keep diseases at bay.

Control your weaknesses and embrace righteousness. Drive worries out of your mind; stay fit and healthy. Believe in your own strengths but have faith in others' capabilities.

Power of Words

5

Have you ever wondered why great men, poets and sages like Buddha, Mahavira, Guru Nanak, Kabir, Rahim, Confucius, Mahatma Gandhi and Vivekananda continue to hold sway over millions long after they have passed away? These men did not possess un- limited wealth or unparalleled military might. They were not emperors, who ruled over massive kingdoms. Nor did they unleash a reign of terror to establish their supremacy over myriad subjects. What then made them immortal?

They were all ordinary mortals, who possessed the great power of speech. Their strength lay in their unique 'armies of thoughts'. Their amazing words were their soldiers. It is the timeless magic of their wisdom that has held people captive for eternity.

True, a 'word' seems like an inconspicuous entity. Yet it possesses an everlastingly supreme strength. It has the ability to transform a life, a society, and a country... nay even the whole world. Words can bring in harmony; they can also trigger mutiny! Like the famous poet Kabir Das succinctly says:

> Why do people glorify words; they have no legs or arms
> Yet one of them can heal, while the other causes harm

The impressive eloquence of these saints has galvanized generations. The world too is full of a host of great literary works and creations!

Acknowledge the power of words and let it influence every aspect of your life. For it is through lessons contained in these words that one acquires a deeper insight into the complexities of life.

Acknowledge the power of words and let it influence every aspect of your life.

While a king is revered only in his own empire, a learned man is venerated the world over!

Price of Civilisation

I can recall a few lines of the celebrated Hindi poet, Agyey:

> Snake, you never became civilised?
> You never learnt to live in cities?
> If I ask you a question, will you answer?
> If I ask you a question, will you answer?
> Then where did you learn to sting?
> Where did you get your poison?

This is no mere satire. The poet's deep anguish over the deteri-
orating city environment is palpable in his scathing commentary on
urbanisation. Long ago, man lived in the wild. Slowly he evolved and
became a social being. Pursuit of science and technology enabled
him and his civilisation to scale enormous heights, but for a price. He
denuded flourishing forests and spewed smoke and other venomous
things in the atmosphere. The raucous noise of automobiles and
factories that he constructed drowned the sweet chirping of birds. He
sullied rivers and choked drains with chemicals. And yet he proclaims
that his civilisation is making progress! Today the world in which we
dwell is full of corruption and crime. And hoarding, bribery and
decadence have become the order of the day. Now, can anyone
interpret civilisation in any other way?

*We are accountable to this earth on which we live, to nature
which sustains us and most importantly, to ourselves.*

If we disagree with the poet's definition, want to retain our respect
for human values and do not want our succeeding generations to
hold us in contempt, we should make it our moral responsibility to
change this very definition. For we are accountable to this earth on
which we live, to nature which sustains us and most importantly, to
ourselves.Only then can we give a new meaning to our civilisation,
society and culture.

Foundation

7

Everyone praises a beautiful building. Little do they realise that
the edifice is a burden on the very foundation on which it stands.
The world sings paeans in praise of beauty and perfume of flowers.
Yet, how many of us think of the seed to which a flower owes its
fragrant existence.

Our life is also similar. Why should we become a burden on others?
Rather, we should make ourselves so capable, complete and strong,

Soul Curry
for you and me

that like the foundation stone of a building, we are equipped to lend support to others. The importance of a strong foundation is quite obvious. Even a gigantic tree draws nourishment from its base – roots. And a diamond, however sturdy, expensive and glistening, can never replace a foundation stone of a building. Mighty are those who provide others an anchor. A hurricane can devastate mansions– but it can never touch foundation stones!

> *The importance of a strong foundation is quite obvious. Even a gigantic tree draws nourishment from its base – roots.*

Lessons from the ignoramus

There is an old saying, which goes something like this:

> *You will run out of knowledge if you try to teach a fool,*
> *For even a hundred tons of soap, will not bleach coal!*

Just as it is futile to bleach coal, similarly it is fruitless to reason out with an ignoramus! True, from time immemorial, the world has always ridiculed the ignorant. But would it surprise you if I say even an ignoramus can teach many a lesson to the wise.

The truth is that a wise man stands to learn much more from a fool than a fool from a wise person. The more we try and teach the foolish the more we realise how ignorant we really are. Their ignorance and foolhardiness is a constant reminder to us as to what we should do and what we should avoid.

> *The truth is that a wise man stands to learn much more from a fool than a fool from a wise person.*

We should learn from the mistakes and experiences of others, particularly from those less knowledgeable than we are. If our experiences are not grounded in reality, our decisions can never be correct.

Everyone makes mistakes, either out of carelessness or ignorance. Unaware, we all behave foolishly at some point of time in our lives. To learn from one's follies is true wisdom, but to repeat the blunder is akin to commiting suicide. No one expects you to actually seek a nitwit and make him your guru. But, yes, we expect a wise person to tap the wisdom hidden amidst the blathering of a fool.

Mirage

In a hot, arid desert, the sand, at a distance, shimmers like water. The thirsty traveller mistakes the spectacle for an oasis. He chases it but in vain. For it is only an illusion. What happens in deserts is also a fact of our everyday life. In reality, we are neither in a desert nor do we trudge on the red-hot sand. Yet, quite often, we reel under different illusions.

Everyone aspires to respect and status, worldly possessions, wealth and fame. Of what use is this opulence if we were to lose our peace of mind, happiness and health? Isn't this a mere illusion? To camouflage our inner weaknesses with a glittering facade is nothing but deception. We sport a pair of gold-framed spectacles with pride

but what we hide behind them is our weak vision. This is the harsh reality of life!

There are countless such examples. Are wealth, property, and status really indispensable? To my mind what is indispensable is a healthy mind and body, and yes – a contented life! Affluence just cannot soothe a mind which is full of discontent, worries, and procrastination.

> *To camouflage our inner weaknesses with a glittering facade is nothing but deception.*

Serene thoughts, a heart full of joy, a clear and firm conscience, a calm mind and robust health contribute in large measure to our outlook of the external world. They change our perception drama- tically. The world seems more beautiful and tranquil. Beyond anyone's imagination!

Determination

10

We nurture beautiful dreams and have multiple desires. We plan passionately and chase grand goals. Lost in a maze of diverse am- bitions, we often find ourselves wandering endlessly in different directions.   We aim for the skies. Result? We end up with nothing. Needlessly, our energy is being channelled in various directions.

> *Success dawns only when we pursue a fixed goal single-mindedly.*

Every individual has the innate ability to fulfill a single objective one at a time. Pursuit of diverse goals dilutes one's spirit. Strengths turn into weaknesses. A focussed approach to life however, helps to augment one's core strengths. What we should therefore aim at is a singular goal.

I recall a Hindi proverb, which means:

Success is certain when the target is fixed.

Dabbling in many a thing leaves all hopes frustrated.

We are flawed if we believe that we can accomplish too many things at one time. One cannot sail in two boats simultaneously. Success dawns only when we pursue a fixed goal single-mindedly. Remember, in a battle, victory always favours the army that has the unity of intent and not one which is large in number.

Losing and Winning

11

As children we have always read and learnt from our elders that there are two sides to life – losing and winning. And, in all earnestness, we have transferred this wealth of knowledge to our next generation. True, every individual dreads failure and is ecstatic at his success. But it is not necessary that winning should always mean material gains and losing be a total fiasco.

> **Sometimes losing can be profitable too. It is so when we shake off our egos, ignorance, fear of criticism, dullness, jealousy and anger.**

Sometimes losing can be profitable too. It is so when we shake off our egos, ignorance, fear of criticism, dullness, jealousy and anger. We benefit enormously by eliminating these bad traits from our personality and thus disprove the oft-repeated adage, which always gives the word 'losing' a negative connotation.

Similarly, winning too is not always synonymous with success. It will not be so till such time as we harbour within us delusion, laziness, deception, fraudulent behaviour and negative thoughts. To acquire such qualities is akin to losing touch with the true meaning of life.

Unfortunately, we have a very narrow perspective of the two concepts. To us losing invariably and essentially means the loss of material success. Conversely, gaining means acquiring all these things. While we may not gain wealth, we can be certain that on the basis of our self-respect, courage, determination, knowledge and unimpeachable character, we can even regain our lost glory.

Risk Taking

Our approach to life is generally very guarded. We do not want to endanger our present or our future. We try to ensure that our career is not threatened. We take decisions using caution. On the whole, our actions do not involve any risk-taking. Well, there is nothing wrong in this approach.

Safety or security is very important in life. But, risk-taking has its own charm. Sometimes, it is necessary to take a few chances, in order to be stupendously successful. What is important is to gamble sensibly. We must not only possess the ability, but also sufficient fortitude and courage to tackle ticklish situations.

This certainly does not mean that we should put our life at stake. We can, however, afford to take a few risks in life. After all, life is an exciting game and only the player who has the grit to handle touch-and-go situations wins.

> *Sometimes, it is necessary to take a few chances, in order to be stupendously successful. What is important is to gamble sensibly.*

Tread the track of life with utmost caution. But let this not deter you from taking giant leaps towards your goals. Excessive caution may reduce your speed to move ahead in life.

Thoughts Maketh the Man

There is an old fable, which talks about a man, who goes to a jungle every day and screams, "Lion! Help!". One day a lion really appears. How much of this is true one does not really know. But the moral of the story is quite clear: Our thoughts greatly influence our circumstances.

Let us not undermine the power of thinking. The man thought of the lion and it surfaced. Evidently, we can make things happen. We need to only conceptualise in our thought–process something that we want to happen.

Positive thinking creates positive vibrations around us. These have a similar kind of effect on people connected with us. A negative thought process impedes progress. And a destructive mentality spells doom. The quality of our thoughts and desires determines what we are and what we ought to be. Like the proverb 'Thoughts maketh the man' indicates, thinking fans desires. Desires influence hopes and ambitions. Ambitions in turn inspire actions. And as we act, so we shape our destiny.

A Worthy Life

From the dawn of humanity, man sought to make new discoveries. He gained expertise in different fields and explored fresh avenues of progress. Technologies and discoveries however, are meaningful only when the motive is altruistic. They should benefit others and contribute in a large measure towards social development.

> *Technologies and discoveries are meaningful only when the motive is altruistic.*

One owes it to oneself to be prosperous and powerful. But worthless is that might which is used to promote only self-interest or to harm others. Acquiring such power is a sheer waste of time. We can never cross the hallowed portals of progress with a bitter mind and a heart full of deceit.

A tree stands mutely in the blistering heat of the afternoon sun, its silence holding a poignant message. A classic giver, it plays to perfection its role of providing shelter to tired travellers, despite adversities.

Remember, true worth lies in being useful to others.

Oneness

Nature is one. There is only one truth in life. We have a single universe, which has a sole creator. The universe harbours one earth. The planet nurtures a vibrant world of diverse flora and fauna, all emanating from a single source – a seed. It is the one and only sun, which shines on all creatures uniformly. The sky above our heads is one. The air we breathe is one. Our soul is unique and so is the Supreme Being.

> *There is only one truth in life. We have a single universe, which has a sole creator.*

We have only one life. And the man, who lives this life with zest, is one. Motherhood is unique. The heart that pumps the fluid of life into our body is also unique. Our mind, a storehouse of astonishing energies, is but one!

Chain Reaction

16

Open the gates of your mind to malice just once, and it is there to stay. Invite bad qualities and you embrace all its friends, kith and kin and kindred spirits. A tendency to steal, idleness, jealousy, contempt, lies, fraud... and more such vices swiftly take a firm root in your mind!

> *Open the gates of your mind to malice just once, and it is there to stay.*

Quite often, people opt for shortcuts to quickly deal with tricky situations. In the long run however, the temptation proves far too expensive. It ignites a chain reaction. It has a cascading effect. To hide one untruth you resort to another and then, to yet another. And then you are lost in a never-ending maze of vices.

Stay Focussed

Wisdom is when you think before you act. Caution is when you think during the action. And when you think after the act it is recklessness. Most of us have a major drawback: we do not predetermine our goal nor do we strive hard to achieve it. We accept meekly whatever comes our way, call it destiny and get down to living it albeit half–heartedly. This is not correct.

> *A person, whose gaze is fixed on his goal does not notice the obstacles that line his path.*

When we do not have a definite goal, we are not ready to take up the challenge. Result? We fail in our endeavour. We are disillusioned. Invariably, we attribute our failure to unfavourable circumstances. When in reality, we just do not possess the resilience to handle difficult situations.

I illustrate this point with a story from the great epic, *Mahabharata*. Dronacharya, the venerable guru of the Pandavas was teaching his students the nuances of archery. During the course of lessons, the guru wanted his students to aim at the eye of a bird that was perched atop a tree. "Tell me what do you see?" he asked his students turn by turn, once each one took aim. One student said he could see the bra-nches of the tree, yet another saw the entire tree. A third could view not only the tree but also the sun that was shining over it.

The Guru then asked Arjuna what he saw. Pat came the reply, "Gurudev, I can see only the bird's eye." Saying this he sent the shaft straight into his target. Arjuna's goal was clear and focussed. And he accomplished it irrespective of all odds: the distance between him and the tree, its swaying branches and the bright sunlight. The moral of the story is simple. A person, whose gaze is fixed on his goal does not notice the obstacles that line his path.

Responsibilities

In life, all of us have to take on responsibilities. Some have more obligations to meet, some less. Many of us attribute our failure to duties thrust on us.

> *Do not run away from responsibilities. They are an integral part of your life. Shoulder them willingly, and with a smile.*

Actually, having to meet one's responsibilities is not the cause of success or failure. It is one's approach to tasks that catapults one to greater heights or seals one's fate. Those who do not shoulder their burden with care, are bound to over balance and may even lose face. Or, the fear of failure may compel them to simply shun responsibility forever.

The wherewithal with which we perform our duty is not important. Our approach is. Means are mere lifeless tools. Our perseverance breathes life into them. Our determination gives them unlimited power. Do not run away from responsibilities. Let them not intimidate you. They are an integral part of your life. Shoulder them willingly, and with a smile. Capitalise on your innate strengths. Face life with courage and conviction. Success will not be far behind.

Personality

Sometimes, I ask myself: "Do people find me attractive? Do they like my appearance?"

Many people associate beauty with outward show. This is what I have to tell them. Beauty is not only an arresting appearance. We may have striking looks. But we may not appeal to people if we are wicked, lack self-confidence and good manners, and if we do not possess good communication skills. Physical beauty alone is insufficient to turn you into an attractive personality.

Evaluate your own strengths and weaknesses. All this needs a pretty straightforward approach.

You may be unattractive, but you may still be noticed. People who meet you may want to appreciate you and even emulate you. Be introspective if you want to be the person of your own dreams. Have a hard look at yourself. Evaluate your own strengths and weaknesses. All this needs a pretty straightforward approach. A guarded approach to life may block good thoughts from flowing in.

But self-evaluation does not mean counting only your faults. Emphasise your positive qualities. Positive thinking can turn vices into virtues. No one is born perfect. So why do we shed tears over our imperfections. Make a beginning. Start analysing yourself. Create a personality of your own – charming, appealing to people and most importantly, one which reflects inner beauty.

Pandora's Box

> *Appreciate the smiles of small children, notice only the good points of others. Your life will always be full of sweetness, peace and satisfaction.*

Psychiatrists compare our mind with an invisible box. From dawn to dusk we work. We pick and choose events and thoughts, memories,

and a plethora of interactions, reactions and transactions and store these in our mind. As night descends and we return home, we bring back with us our prize possessions. Some of these leave a fragrant trail, while others raise a stink.

Life is difficult for those who revel in criticism of others, harbour negative thoughts and nurse a grudge or a feeling of jealousy towards others.

But for those who love to bask in the soft glow of the sun, enjoy the sweet chirping of birds, the resonance of temple bells and *azans* from mosques, it is a pleasure trip.

Appreciate the smiles of small children, notice only the good points of others. Your life will always be full of sweetness, peace and satisfaction.

Duty Lies in Action

21

For a person who wants to be heard there is a no dearth of listeners. Lakhs will give advice, thousands will pay heed to it and perhaps hundreds will understand its real meaning. But when it comes to actually doing things, there are very few who will answer the call of duty. You can literally count them on your fingertips.

> *To act is akin to meditation, and the path leads to liberation. Blessed are those who acknowledge that their duty lies in action.*

The crux of the problem is that most of us take interest in either talking big or simply listening to others. But when it comes to actually performing the deed, we vanish from the scene. We forget what our scriptures have taught us over the centuries. To act is akin to meditation, and the path leads to liberation. Blessed are those who acknowledge that their duty lies in action.

Everybody wants to reach the top, but only he who strives to reach it can do so. A bird cannot enjoy the expanse of the sky by merely sitting in its nest, similarly an individual cannot scale great heights if he is not willing to act.

Right Gift

Forgiveness is the best gift you could give to your enemy and for a friend, gift a place in your heart! Present your opponents with a favour. For a child, it is right advice. For a father it is respect and for a mother, our achievements that will make her heart swell with pride.

To make others happy we need to be happy ourselves.

Take for instance, a flame. Not only does it illuminate its surroundings but also transfers its radiance to a thousand lamps. Similarly, the greatness of a person not only benefits him, but also inspires others to emulate the act. In order to set an example to others, we need to have our own house in order first. To make others happy we need to be happy ourselves. One cannot illuminate the world when our own life is enveloped in darkness.

initiatives

There is a Chinese proverb, which says that all big things have small beginnings. I believe that taking initiative is the first step towards success. Yet, we often look up to a guardian angel to prod and guide us to take up the challenges of life. And till that happens we live in a constant state of inertia.

True inspiration has an important role to play in our life. And rightly so! Great men, saints, seers and philosophers, social workers and patriots, all have been a source of inspiration for us and will continue to be so in times to come. But in order to be successful it is we who have to take the first step. It is this very step that will take us closer to our

goal. A combination of our inner motivation and external inspiration will spur us towards success. Then there is no goal that we cannot achieve, no dream that we cannot realise!

> *A combination of our inner motivation and external inspiration will spur us towards success.*

Move On

There is an unwritten rule that what does not move forward should be left behind. Where there is no progress, there is regression, decadence and destruction. Clearly, if one is not willing to charge forward, progress stops right there.

Our life owes its existence to fresh air. And it ceases to exist when our heart stops beating. Hence speed is the name of the game and is the true meaning of life. The *Vedas* say, "march ahead." A person who refuses to follow the edict remains static in life. Lady luck turns her face away from one who refrains from the challenges of life. Destiny favours the man who is hardworking and who is constantly on the move. For movement is growth. And growth signifies evolution.

The importance of intelligence

Just because we are born human, it does not mean that we are courageous. Courage does not automatically make us deserving. And, even if we have the skills and knowledge to make it big, it does not promise success. Success may not always be a sign of progress. Progress does not indicate wealth.

> *A hundred fools are far superior to a man, who like his accumulated wealth, locks up his intelligence in a safe!*

Opulence does not guarantee the art of speaking. And even when one acquires this ability, it does not mean that our hearts overflow with love. However, even if we acquire the aforesaid qualities but lack intelligence, all these qualities are rendered useless.

Animals are the greatest of all beings. Amongst these, the greatest are the ones who possess intelligence. And amongst them man is supreme. The one who possesses sharp intellect is superior to all his fellow beings. And success follows the person who puts his intelligence to good use.

But a hundred fools are far superior to a man, who like his accumulated wealth, locks up his intelligence in a safe!

Rules

You must have often stood on a beach watching waves surging towards the sand with speed. Turn by turn they come, dash against the shore in rhythmic swirls, and then return to the sprawling expanse of water. This has been their routine from the time the world was created. Yet they show no sign of fatigue. The shore's affection for the surf too seems eternal. Each moment it welcomes a new wave, arms stretched out lovingly, and with the same undying fervour.

Since the beginning of the cosmos, the sun has been setting the sky ablaze with gold-red dawns. It dispels with its rays the gloom of the night. Then night falls and darkness envelops the world once more. The next day again is a new day, a new beginning. This is an endless cycle, a never-ending pattern of nature's creation, which has been unfolding for myriad centuries, rhythmically, unfalteringly, and uncomplainingly.

These natural phenomena have their own significance. They help the earth to maintain a balance. Both the sun and waves are outstanding examples of courage and fortitude. They teach us to play our role to perfection, unruffled by events and adversities. For grit and diligence, the qualities they symbolize, are but harbingers of success. That is the true spirit of life.

> *Like sunrise engulfs darkness, courage helps one to surmount suffering.*

Like sunrise engulfs darkness, courage, helps one to surmount suffering. A wave, which untiringly washes the shoreline, symbolizes hardwork. Efforts are not made in vain, it says. For a wave sometimes leaves a legacy. Some precious pearls from the sea!

The Pathway to Success

27

The passage to success is not a bed of roses. Invariably, it is lined with countless worries. You encounter failure at every nook and corner. Problems, often unsurmountable, block your progress. Illusion and confusion dot every crossing. Kith and kin impede your pace. The undulating terrain has disappointments downhill and obligations uphill. Family is an important checkpost on this trail, pause here you must before you start again.

A vehicle called willpower can help you cross these hurdles. This has valour for wheels, sweat and blood for fuel, duty for engine and faith at the steering. Enthusiasm provides you with the much-needed speed. Your toolbox has courage sprinkled with focus and zeal. Drive intelligently while chasing your goal, you can travel on your road to success with a great deal of ease.

> *A vehicle called willpower has valour for wheels, sweat and blood for fuel, duty for engine and faith at the steering.*

'if'

28

> *Plentiful words were coined by the pen, only to be rehearsed and repeated by men.*
> *'If' is one such word, which make people whine, invariably sending shivers down their spine.*
> *The word is so wicked that it has destroyed our peace, stalled our actions and spoiled our bliss.*
> *It brings displeasure, distress and misery. It hinders progress, duty and charity.*

Of all the words coined so far the one that has caused the most grief to mankind is the word 'If'.

People who get trapped in the 'ifs and buts' syndrome, spend more than half their life whining about what would have happened 'if only they had done this, or had not done that.'

I want to illustrate this point with an old folk tale. Once there was a woman who used to sell curd. She carried it in an earthen pot on her head. One day, on her way to the market she started daydreaming: "What if the king's convoy passes this way... He will see me and make me his queen. I will then be able to rule over everyone. And if someone asks me for something, I will say, 'No, never.'" With that she tossed her head stylishly from one side to the other. The pot fell down and broke into pieces. Therefore, you should never entertain this venomous word. It possesses the power to ruin life.

Like a termite the word 'If' weakens your ability to act. It makes you feel you are incomplete. It will not let you be happy nor enable you to be completely satisfied.

> *Like a termite the word 'If' weakens your ability to act.*
> *It makes you feel you are incomplete.*

Have full faith in yourself, not in your destiny. Let fate follow its own course. You enjoy what you can achieve through your actions, efforts and hard work!

Castles in the Air

Man has always given more importance to the real world around him as against the imaginary one. But, sometimes a dream is a source of inspiration which heralds a change around you. It is a seed from which is born a brave new world. You cannot translate all your dreams into reality. But they can act as a foundation stone for a glorious future.

Man's moon-mania is the best example of his flights of fancy. Man dreamt of conquering the moon. And sure enough, he set foot on it.

There does exist a gulf between the world of fantasy and the real one. But reveries enable a man to achieve desires, which are seemingly impossible to fulfil.

> *You cannot translate all your dreams into reality. But they can act as a foundation stone for a glorious future.*

People generally poke fun at those who build castles in the air. There is no harm in doing that. But our effort should not be fruitless. We should have these castles firmly rooted in reality!

The Value of Experience

30

Any action has only two conclusions: success or failure. If the effort is successful, we gain something. On the other hand, if we fail we incur a loss. But this assumption is wrong. Efforts are never wasted. We may not have achieved our goal. But the experience, which we gain in the bargain, deepens our understanding. It is a reward, which comes free with every effort that we put in.

You cannot collect experience from books. You cannot buy it in the bazaar either. You cannot create it. Experience comes through effort, hard work and penance.

With every effort, your wealth of experience multiplies manifold. I agree you have to possess some ability and skill to achieve success. Sometimes however, experience compensates for lack of abilities, and you are able to taste the sweet fruit of success!

Quality of Life

We are blessed with a human life. But this life does not really belong to us. We must be aware of the fact that our life will end, some day or the other. Therefore, as long as we live, we should put it to good use. It is not important how long you live. What is significant is the manner in which you live, the kind of actions you perform during your stay on this planet.

Living is not merely breathing in fresh air. Every breath should bring with it fresh thoughts, ideas and goals. The incessant beating of the heart sustains our body. It should also infuse in the system a new vigour to help us overcome our problems. The fluid of life that gushes through our blood vessels should carry with it courage. Every step that we take should spell a new hope. Our eyes should reflect a new dream, better opportunity and a new goal. That is what living is all about!

> *Living does not merely mean existing. It is the quality of life and not the quantity that is important. Life ultimately means moving ahead and proving yourself in the face of difficulties.*

Contentment is a state of mind. He who has clarity of thought performs extremely well and achieves satisfaction. Living does not merely mean existing. It is the quality of life and not quantity that is important. Life ultimately means moving ahead and proving yourself in the face of difficulties.

Emulating and imitating

Everyone has a role model, from which he seeks inspiration. He strives to emulate that person. But it is one thing to pick good qualities from someone and quite different to imitate him blindly. There is a world of difference between mere imitation and lessons that are truly learnt.

A hardworking person learns from others. He combines these lessons with his own actions. A person who copies others blindly lacks faith in himself. Replication is successful only when it is intelligently done and has an original flavour. It has to stand the test of time. We have to apply it to our day to day life. Only then does it lead to progress.

Mere imitation does not guarantee success. Others can only inspire us. But the hardwork is ours. The message is simple. A vulture cannot be a lion by merely imitating it!

Think Right

Swami Vivekananda had said, '*Thoughts are the seeds of action*'. Action originates in thought. Our deeds take shape in our mind first as thoughts. The moment you sow seeds of thoughts you also create the possibility of converting them into action. This is the first step towards progress. Hence we should think of new ideas and have productive thoughts.

An idea is extremely short-lived. Hence it is best to take action as soon as it blossoms. Otherwise you might just lose it or it may fade away into oblivion. Not only must you implement your ideas but also ensure that your thoughts remain alive and evergreen.

> *An idea is extremely short-lived. Hence it is best to take action as soon as it blossoms.*

According to psychologists ninety-five per cent of the people are capable of much more than what they imagine they are capable of. We must tap our true strength, abilities and courage. Then nothing can stop us from attaining the success that we dream of.

Satisfaction

In a gathering of learned men, a question was once raised: What is the most beautiful thing on earth? Most of the learned men present opined that appearance, children, nature, music, sunrise were among the most beautiful things in the universe. But one wise man differed from the rest. He believed that the most beautiful thing in this universe was contentment. And then, on reflection, everyone agreed with him.

A man may accumulate unlimited wealth and build numerous palaces. But all these are useless if he lacks peace of mind. As I have said before, happiness is a state of mind. You may find it in a palace or in a tiny cottage. Our real wealth is our satisfaction and it reflects in our thoughts and actions. We should be happy with what we have achieved and what we will do in the future. Herein lies our true happiness.

> **Happiness is a state of mind. You may find it in a palace or in a tiny cottage.**

But do not be satisfied with little and curtail your creativity. Do not curb your thought process. That will halt your progress. Always aim for a bigger picture.

I do not agree with this saying I now quote:

So what if a python lies stupefied or a bird does not work,
Daas Maluka says Lord Rama is the supreme benefactor.

This means that even if you do not work there is a supreme being who will provide you with everything. This is wrong thinking. I firmly believe that we must exploit every opportunity that comes our way. We must sincerely strive to achieve each goal. And work hard to do well in life. We should be satisfied with what we get as a result of our efforts. Only then will each achievement give us true happiness and peace of mind.

A Dutiful Son and an Errant Son

There is an old saying, which goes something like this: *It is as futile to bequeath your wealth to a devoted child as it is to an errant one.* While the latter squanders his inheritance, the former possesses the ability to create his own empire.

True, the main focus of this adage seems wealth. But read in between the lines. What it basically does is differentiates between a good and bad child. It points out that a good son is capable of building his own future and on his own merit.

Soul Curry
for you and me

We look forward to a splendid tomorrow. We should not however, overlook what lies behind our success. It is the struggle of our parents, who have sacrificed their present to ensure a secure future for us.

We cannot even imagine repaying our parents for all that they have done for us. What can we give them? They have nurtured us and showered us with the best values and qualities. They have prepared us to take up the challenges of life. This debt cannot be repaid. But there is something we can do for them. We can make them feel proud of our achievements.

> *We should not overlook what lies behind our success.*
> *It is the struggle of our parents, who have sacrificed*
> *their present to ensure a secure future for us.*

importance of Being Organised

When we take a hard look at our life we notice that it is in a perpetual state of turmoil. Everything appears to be scattered and disorganised. Why does this happen? We have the means, the ability and the time to hit our target. Yet, we are not able to achieve that degree of success which we desire.

The reasons are not far to seek. What we lack is proper management. Without proper planning, there can be no success. The importance of organisation is underlined by the way our body functions.

> ▍ *Without proper planning, there can be no success.* ▍

Our body is made up of a multitude of parts with varied functions. Yet as a unit, it functions in an entirely organised manner. The system keeps the body clock ticking. Life ebbs the moment this clock comes to a halt. We need to evolve a system like this in our day-to-day life. Life gets difficult sans proper planning. In one sense, organisation means knowledge and the lack of it, ignorance. Try to achieve something in an organised manner. Even a small effort will reap a big harvest.

The Past, Present and Future

Our past never returns so why regret it and the future is an unsolved mystery, so why think of it. There is a beautiful couplet, which brings out the poignancy of this thought.

> *Do not think of the past.*
> *Whatever happened has happened.*
> *Once upon a time, in the bright, blue sky.*
> *There was a beautiful, dazzling star.*
> *One day, it fell out and quietly vanished*
> *from the scene.*
>
> *Behold the vast expanse of sky.*
> *Stars have fallen... they have gone far*
> *Pose these stars a simple query; has heaven got over their loss,*
> *ever felt sorry?*
> *What has gone is a thing of the past, why regret it, why should*
> *we worry.*

Between the past and the future lies our present. We can mould it in whichever way we please. While doing so we should learn from our past and keep in mind the possibilities of the future.

We must act wisely in the present. Then we will never have to regret the past or worry about the future. Yet we often ruin our present, first by weeping over what has happened and then by living in fear about what is to come.

We must act wisely in the present. Then we will never have to regret the past or worry about the future.

Instead of doing so, we must make every effort to keep our present alive. It is the biggest reality of our lives. Hence it is essential that we gain absolute control over our present.

Life, a Struggle

There are different definitions of life. While some have called it a stage, others have compared it to an ever-rolling stream. Life for some is a testing ground of all their actions, while for some others it is the first step towards salvation. For cynics however, life is a "long sentence of sorrows punctuated by happiness". They believe that its peeves overshadow its pleasures.

For those who agree with this definition, life is really a sentence, a curse. Only cowards think in this manner. They are aware that problems are an integral part of life. But they turn a blind eye to this fact. Have you ever heard these people pray? They urge the Almighty to make their life trouble–free. They want a crisis-free life and ask for readymade solutions to their problems.

Life is a struggle. Difficulties are an essential part of it.

But this approach is wrong and is not in tune with reality. Life is a struggle. Difficulties are an essential part of it. So, whenever we pray

we should ask God to give us the strength to face the ups and downs of life boldly. We must ask for capabilities to conquer difficulties and courage to overcome hardship. This *is* the truth of life.

Can you find gold without sifting through sand?
Can you get to a garden without walking through thorns?
An encounter with ills of life should not leave you cold
For you cannot reach the courtyard, without crossing the threshold.

Right Moment

39

Once a painter drew a portrait of 'Time'. It was a beautiful figure with a smile on its face and outstretched arms. It had a thick mop of hair in front, but was completely bald from behind.

The artist had his own reasoning. When the 'right' moment arrives, he said, it beckons you with open arms. You control it provided you grab it by the hair in front. Should you let it slip you can never catch it again. Its baldpate will deter you from holding it firmly. And then the situation goes out of your control.

Wonderful opportunities do not come often. In fact, opportunity knocks at your door only once. Do not lose time in inviting it in. If it goes away it is lost forever. And then misfortune takes its place. It knocks at our door incessantly till we are forced to open the door and let it in.

Don't let an opportunity slip by. That is the key to success.

Grab the opportunities that come your way. Or else you are in for trouble. And then you will have only yourself to blame.

Don't let an opportunity slip by. That is the key to success.

Self-Esteem and Ego

40

Ego and self-respect are two words we often come across. Both these words seem mundane. But both possess the power to give a new meaning to our life. While self-esteem signifies progress and success, ego is the beginning of our end.

A person who has self-respect breaks but never bends. He never falters in the face of the gravest crisis. On the other hand ego is destructive. It makes a person lose his balance, even his sanity.

Ego annihilates our good qualities and capabilities, our intelligence and aptitude. It causes a complete degeneration of our personality. Self-respect is another name for walking tall. The world looks up to those who do not compromise on their self-respect.

Self-esteem instills self-confidence. It inculcates independent thinking. It showers on us glory, progress and many achievements.

Four Types of People

Here is an interesting saying:

He who knows not and knows not that he knows not is
foolish.
Stay away from him.
He who knows not but knows that he knows not is simple.
Teach him.
He who knows but knows not that he knows is asleep.
Wake him up.
And he who knows and knows that he knows is a
learned man.
Make him your teacher.

This means that a person, who is ignorant and is unaware of this fact, lives under a veil of misunderstanding throughout his life. It is pointless to try and teach him anything. Avoid him.

The second individual is ignorant, but he is aware of his shortcomings. This one is simple. Teach him. Show him the light of knowledge.

The person in the third category is educated but he is not aware about his potentialities. He is sleeping. You need to shake him up from his slumber and make him aware of his strengths.

> *Be aware of what you know and what you do not. You can then be your own guide.*

The scholarly man is fully conscious of his intellectual prowess. He should be venerated. Make him your guru, guide and philosopher. Be aware of what you know and what you do not. Get rid of your inadequacies. Comprehend your potential. You can then be your own guide.

Enthusiasm

Quite often we have the talent, expertise and the means to scale great heights. Yet success always eludes us. Our goal seems far off. There is a reason for this. We do not seem to have enough enthusiasm to pursue our goal. Apathy clouds our latent talent. Indifference affects our approach to a task. We can work to the best of our abilities only when we are completely motivated.

> *We can work to the best of our abilities only when we are completely motivated.*

Fervour energises us. It ignites within us a new thought process. Many great men attribute their stupendous success to their unmatched zeal and not so much to their competence. Wise men observe, 'Ageing is a state of mind'. Grey hair should not dampen your spirits. Let wrinkles, a sign of old age, cover your face. They should never encroach upon your zest.

Victory and Defeat

What determines your victory or defeat? It is one of these two words– bravery and cowardice. Courage is what assures you of victory. And you are vanquished if you lack courage.

> *The fear of failure is more dangerous than failure itself.*

The fear of failure is more dangerous than failure itself. It devastates courage. It destroys your efforts. People who rise above this negative emotion find that the possibilities of success are tremendous, and can indeed transform their dreams into reality.

Power of the Subliminal

Our galaxy is a small speck in the whole universe. It is replete with several big planets, stars and other heavenly bodies. The earth, on which we dwell, is huge. But it is nothing compared to the vastness of space. Where does man fit in this race for supremacy?

In fact, it is worthless to even draw comparisons between man and the earth in relation to size. If one considers the vast canvas of the universe, we are so insignificant.

What then is this magical power, which has enabled us to rule over the vast expanse of nature for billions of years? It is our brain, our mind. It is with this power of thinking that a human being aspires to explore the unknown world. This is why we need to tap our inner resources. We need to trap the new thoughts that emanate in our

mind. We have to come up with new ideas and discoveries. Otherwise it will not be long before our grey matter turns into an insignificant appendage of our body. I am not really exaggerating when I say that our ideas outnumber the stars in the sky.

Hard Work Brings Success

Fortune favours the person who works hard. This is the undisputed law of nature. Nothing is impossible for a person who is willing to put in the required effort. Like the old Rajasthani saying, depicting a scene from the great epic Ramayana, goes:

> *Lord Rama asks Sugreeva how far is Lanka.*
> *Prompt comes the reply:*
> *For those dull and languid it is far, far away.*
> *But for those full of vigour just a stone's throw away.*

The moral of the story is simple. Success comes to those who work hard. Those who wander along the beach find conches and shells. But those who dare to venture into the depth of the ocean discover precious pearls.

Tolerance

During the Second World War, the Japanese army had enforced an interesting rule. Anyone who wanted to make a complaint could do so only after ten days. They had to write it down and drop it in a complaint box.

> *Sleep over your differences. Many will fly away leaving the proverbial complaint box perpetually empty. For all you know there could be letters therein not of protest but of love.*

Believe me, when the box was opened ten days after this rule was framed, it was found to be completely empty!

It is a fascinating tale and one that has a close relevance to our social life. If we live our lives with a little courage, patience and tolerance, we may tend to ignore several of our difficulties. We may find them insignificant.

This is the secret behind a successful married life as well. Sleep over your differences. Many will fly away leaving the proverbial complaint box perpetually empty. For all you know there could be letters therein not of protest but of love.

Bonding

The words, 'I' and 'we' are not mere pronouns. These are words, which symbolise peace, happiness and harmony in one's family life. Behold the words 'I', 'mine', and 'myself'. These are tainted with conceit and selfishness. They do give one a distinct identity. But the danger is that they also fuel arrogance. One is fully immersed in oneself. There is no world beyond the self.

But the word 'we' signifies team spirit. It instills a sense of belonging and a feeling of camaraderie. It is the essence of

happiness and a blissful married life. The key word is 'ours', not 'me' or 'mine'.

The words, 'we' and 'ours' stir a bond of closeness. They contain a promise of a better and safe future.

If letters can teach one the lesson of love, then from the two-lettered word 'we', one learns about oneness and bonding. They stand for a happy social and family life.

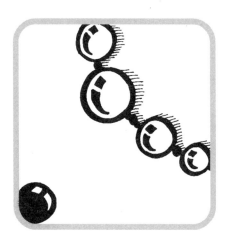

Building Your Family

The foundation of a family is not laid merely when people live under the same roof. It is bound together by strong ties, unbreakable bonds and a promise of a safe future.

> *Our every effort must be focussed on keeping the family together and helping it progress in life.*

It is for this reason that our society and culture have always emphasised the importance of a unified family. It is not only a great support system but it also plays a big role in an individual's success and accomplishments.

Every individual in a family is like a pillar. He should strive to make the family structure strong. He should create an impregnable wall around it to protect it from calamities. An addition of a new member may not much alter a family's makeup. But his exit would, unquestionably! The family may break apart, or just disintegrate.

Hence, our relationship with each other ought to be strong, and our faith in each other unshakeable. Our every effort must be focussed on keeping the family together and helping it progress in life. Such a family is a microcosm of the whole world.

The Beauty of Relationships

This world consists of lakhs and crores of people. It is indeed surprising how one person forms a relationship with another. An ordinary relationship is transformed into an extraordinary one because it rises above caste or class, creed or religion or any other social constraints. Whether it is the relationship between friends, husband and wife or lovers, it is necessary that we keep its warmth alive. A relationship is as delicate as a thread. A small jerk can split it apart. You can undoubtedly tie it together again, but it is not the same: You will find a knot in it.

> *Whether it is the relationship between friends, husband and wife or lovers, it is necessary that we keep its warmth alive.*

There is a reason behind the formation of any relationship, an unusual coming together, a tough test and a comparing and a mingling of minds. We may have small differences in any relationship. But if we want them to grow stronger day by day, we should not let our minds grow apart. A relationship is most beautiful when there are no differences in it.

Motive

The importance of a thing is often judged by the purpose for which it is being used. Take for instance a dagger. A criminal uses it to commit a murder. But, in the hands of a doctor, the same knife turns into a life-saving surgical instrument. A nation swells with pride beholding a soldier guarding the borders with his gun. But the deadly weapon becomes a source of terror when carried by a criminal.

In both the situations quoted above, while the means used to accomplish the goal are the same, the motive is different. Just as a sinful   intention undermines the importance of a resource, likewise a wrong motive not only brings us disgrace, but also ruins our life.

> *A wrong motive not only brings us disgrace, but also ruins our life.*

Even dubious means serve great causes when the motive is good. Take for instance, poison. This is a deadly substance. But when used in the right manner it can be used to make life-saving drugs.

Husband and Wife

Doors, windows, walls and a roof make a house. But it is the husband and wife who transform it into a home. Why does this happen? The answer is simple. It is not only the husband and wife who live in the house. They bring along with them love, affection, and companionship, and create a deep bond based on mutual faith. These emotions motions give their nest a special significance and uphold its sanctity.

Husband and wife. These are not merely two words relegated to the pages of a dictionary. It is a great concept, a strong, sustainable relationship based on a solid foundation of trust and complete surrender to each other. It is this devotion that keeps the relationship between two completely alien people alive. It binds them for the rest of their life.

Marriage

Marriage is a social institution, which not only unites two people, but also their families, cultures and societies from which they hail. Civilisation undoubtedly began with the advent of man. But it is the institution of marriage that has created its social fabric. Matrimony has provided societies with stability and has maintained their unity. The environment helps the earth to maintain its balance, the institution of marriage maintains the balance in our society.

Marriage signifies growth. It makes a human being complete – mentally, physically and spiritually!

Matrimony

Marriage is an interesting concept. It is a vibrant relationship, in which both the wife and husband are perpetually at loggerheads.

She accuses him of absentmindedness. He feels she is cantankerous. She often laments that her husband never listens to her, while he maintains that she never lets him have his say!

Once, a woman complained of her spouse's habit of talking in his sleep to a doctor. The physician examined her husband and gave his diagnosis. He told the wife, "Madam, your husband will get rid of his habit provided the poor man gets a chance to speak during the day!"

> *The relationship between the spouses should be based on mutual love. There can be differences but never a rift.*

Every human relationship, specially the one between husband and wife, has its bitter-sweet moments. This is what gives their love intensity. The relationship between the spouses should be based on mutual love. There can be differences but never a rift. The husband and wife are like the two wheels of the vehicle of life. Together they help it to move forward. Their mindsets need to match to avoid an unpleasant journey.

Good and Evil

There are two kinds of people in this world: those who are good and those who are bad. The righteous people bring glory to themselves and to the society of which they are a part and parcel. But those people, who have knowingly or unknowingly chosen the path of dishonesty, have to confront difficulties.

> *Every individual has the capacity to distinguish between good and evil. It is also a fact that we need a friend, philosopher and guide to show us the right path.*

One question is often raised. Why do we tread the wrong path, when our elders have always encouraged us to embrace virtues, teachers have always guided us properly and wellwishers have given us sound advice? We do it because we labour under the illusion that we are superior to others. We disregard others' advice.

Every individual has the capacity to distinguish between good and evil. It is also a fact that we need a friend, philosopher and guide to show us the right path. Even the legendary Ekalavya felt the need of a guru to master the art of archery. So what if his teacher was in the form of a statue!

Keeping Pace

Speed is an essential element of this cosmos. Speed is what makes life tick. It is what makes the world run, and time flow. Without pace, progress is impossible.

The earth continuously rotates on its axis and revolves around the sun. Time, like an ever-rolling stream, flows and one never realises when seconds turn into minutes, minutes into hours, hours into days,

days into years and years into centuries. We have to understand the rhythm of time and keep pace with it. Those who move ahead with time know where they have to go. They are the achievers!

Success by Another Name

Success does not come easily to anyone. You have to struggle hard to emerge triumphant. It is not possible to steer to safety a boat which is caught up in a storm, just by sitting on the banks.

Similarly you cannot move ahead in life without taking up the challenges posed by the adversities that line your way. Even gold gets its sheen after being purified in fire. Henna, a natural dye, attains a deep red shade only after being ground. Brace yourself for a tussle with life should you want to find its true meaning.

> *A tryst with adversities of life enhances our self-confidence and our spiritual strength.*

Realistically speaking, struggle is another name for growth. A tryst with adversities of life enhances our self-confidence and our spiritual strength. We mature as a person. Like we have a lifeline on our palm, which is a symbol of a long or a short life, our hands too should sport

a 'line of struggle' to enable us to lead our life on our own terms. Isn't success, after all, another name for struggle?

Practicing and Preaching

The easiest thing in the world is to give advice to others. And the most difficult thing is to practice what we preach. Notice that there is a world of difference between what one says and what one actually does. A person's speech should be consonant with his actions. We become lacklustre if we do not practice what we preach. We have no moral grounds to sermonise if our actions are not in harmony with our words.

Waxing eloquence does not make a man great. He becomes great when he sets an example to others by living up to his words. It is this commitment that distinguishes an ordinary person from an extraordinary one. And then you can expect spectacular achievements from such a man!

A Fistful of Hopes

It is an age-old belief that man is born empty-handed and departs from this world... also empty-handed. But this is an illusion. For, as a newborn baby, a man brings with him, in his tightly closed fists, a lot of hopes and potentialities. He brings happiness for those who are close to him.

And when he leaves the world, he does not go empty-handed. He takes with him the credit for all his achievements, the love of his people and the respect and blessings he has garnered in his life.

The Greatest Good

Our nation has always held duty as most important. And all of us perform deeds in our own specific style. Then why is it that some men remain ordinary mortals while others achieve greatness? There is a reason for this.

> *Expand the scope of your actions, work for the benefit of others. This approach gives our life a new meaning.*

Some people are self-centred and do what benefits only them. Every step that they take is only in their own interest. Rarely do they think of others and that is why they do not rise above the ordinary. Great are those who seek social good. They work for the benefit and happiness of the majority and never for personal gain.

Self-aggrandisement limits our thought process and consequentially our actions. It dwarfs our vision and restricts our horizon.

Expand the scope of your actions, work for the benefit of others. This approach gives our life a new meaning. We think anew. Life, after all, is about lending a helping hand to the poor and needy!

inner Resource

If we have courage, we need no friends. Courage and determination are our greatest friends. If we have the power to think rationally, we need not flip through great works of literature. Our sagacity is our best guide. And if we have knowledge, we need no embellishments. Knowledge is more precious than the world's most expensive treasure.

> *Knowledge is more precious than the world's most expensive treasure.*

A person who radiates inner beauty does not require external trappings to make him look attractive. People will not mistake a crow for an eagle merely because it perches on the palace dome like the latter. A person's internal qualities determine his exterior. And his greatness is entirely due to these very qualities.

Present Minded

Past mistakes hold important lessons for our future. But we should not brood over those blunders and make our present miserable. There is nothing wrong in planning for the future. But we should not ruin our present by worrying about the future.

For us, our 'present' should be most important. It enables us to rectify all our past mistakes. It carries in its womb a promise of a better tomorrow. Hence it is often said, *'The wise are those who do not think of the past or worry about the future. They take the present as it comes and finish all their work in time.'*

To control your life, it is not necessary to concentrate on your future. Get a grip on your present for that is the only thing under your control.

Soul Curry
for you and me

Mere Parroting

There is an old story about a man who used to frequently warn his parrot not to fall victim to a scheming hunter. The man explained to his pet the hunter's *modus operandi* in detail. How the hunter would spread his net and then scatter grains to allure him. The parrot repeated his words time and again. One day however, the worst fears of his owner came true. The hunter spread his net and enticed the bird with grains. Despite regular coaching by his owner, the bird got trapped. The story seems funny. But ponder over it for sometime. We too may have behaved in this fashion on many occasions in the past.

Like the parrot, mankind has learnt many things for many centuries: we have been taught to be truthful, self-confident, and to face failure boldly. For some reason we cannot apply the knowledge in our real lives at the relevant time. We seem to lack desire, strength and determination to do this. Our determination is what protects us from calamities and temptations. It is what ensures our success.

Planning

To be successful, you need much more than ability, self-confidence, resources and a goal. You need better planning.

> *A well-thought out plan of action enables man to accomplish things which seem impossible at the first glance.*

Several smaller countries in the world have made great progress purely because of sound planning. A well-thought out plan of action enables man to accomplish things which seem impossible at the first glance. Remember him walking on the moon and you will understand the importance of this logic. Careful planning always yields good results. Conversely, lack of it is likely to spell failure.

We cannot foresee our future. But a well-conceptualised plan provides us a glimpse of what is in store for us. And this is what planning is all about.

Motivation

In the great war of Mahabharata, Arjuna scored a victory over Karna, even though the latter was far superior in the game of warfare. People attribute this to the matchless competence of Arjuna's charioteer, Lord Krishna.

All through the battle, Lord Krishna infused Arjuna with enthusiasm and confidence with his sermons of the Gita, and motivated him to victory. On the other hand Karna's charioteer, Shalya, could not inspire confidence in the warrior at all. Instead, he worked overtime to break down Karna's spirit. He spoke about Arjuna's prowess and hinted that a victory against him was impossible. Naturally, Karna lost the battle and his life too.

The word Shalya means doubt, reservation. And these normally enter our mind through Karna or our ears! Hesitation and insecurities severely impede our progress. While faith in our abilities and self-confidence catapults us to the top.

> *Hesitation and insecurities severely impede our progress.*

State of Mind

Victory and defeat, success and failure, loss and gain are states of mind. Or you could call them the two sides of the same coin.

The victor is not the only one who attains his goal. I would also call a person who leaves no stone unturned to reach his goal a victor, irrespective of whether he wins or loses. The person who takes his defeat in his stride and learns from his past mistakes, is a winner too!

Clear Conscience

If you have a clear conscience you have attained salvation even though you are very much a part and parcel of this illusory world. You may have the gift of the gab or even sophisticated manners. But unless it is coupled with probity, both the attributes will not earn you satisfaction and peace of mind. Such a person is not happy from within and is unable to make others happy.

> *If you have a clear conscience you have attained salvation even though you are very much a part and parcel of this illusory world.*

Purity of mind is a prerequisite to attain happiness in life. This can happen provided you free your mind of negative thoughts and emotions like anger, jealousy, contempt for others and excessive passion for material comforts. You can then view life differently. Life is simpler and much better if your deeds are transparent.

Woman Power

We have been hearing and reading a lot about woman power right from the time we were children. But have we ever tried to comprehend this power, about which a lot has been spoken in our holy scriptures and epics. No, I do not think we have even made an attempt to know what woman power is all about.

All of us have seen our mothers, sisters, wives and daughters making supreme sacrifices, all sorts of compromises and leading a life of complete surrender. We have often misconstrued their goodness for weakness. What we perceive as weakness is actually a sign of great mental strength. It is on account of this strength that women willingly undergo hardships for their beloved ones, and with a smile.

The modern woman is trying to give a new meaning to this power. She is making her presence felt in every walk of life. From the kitchen to the computer lab, her journey has been long but very interesting and fruitful.

> *What we perceive as weakness is actually a sign of great mental strength. It is on account of this strength that women willingly undergo hardships for their beloved ones, and with a smile.*

Dreams

We love to dream. And everyone should dream. I am not talking about day–dreaming, but those grand dreams which compel a man to devote his whole life to making them come true.

I always tell the younger generation to nurture mighty dreams so that they will try their best to fulfil them. When you step into reality from the world of fantasy, you come to a beautiful turning in life, where new vistas open up for you. You have new opportunities knocking at your door. After all, dreams are meant to be realised.

The Human Reservoir

When water from a reservoir flows in a controlled manner, it is a boon to mankind. It irrigates fields and quenches the thirst of human beings. But when the dam impounding this water gives way, the life–giving fluid gushes out forcefully, leaving a trail of death and destruction.

> *A greedy mind destroys your potentialities and corrodes abilities.*

A human mind is also like a reservoir. When it is calm, it sharpens a person's skills and contributes towards his progress and happiness. A greedy mind on the contrary, destroys your potentialities and corrodes abilities. It makes you a completely different person.

Hence, determination is the key to success. A firm mind makes life move in a smooth and determined manner.

A greedy mind destroys your potentialities and corrodes abilities.

inner Voice

We respect other people. That is the way it should be. But we must also respect ourselves. What I am saying here is slightly different but relevant. Self-esteem triggers within you a process of self-purification. It brings you closer to your soul. You can peek into the realm of your mind. You can hear your inner voice, which praises you for the right actions and rebukes you for the wrong deeds. It tells you, in no uncertain terms, whether the expectations you have about yourself are justified or not. Our conscience guides our actions and charts out the future course of events.

> *Self-esteem triggers within you a process of self-purification. It brings you closer to your soul.*

Sages have also underlined the importance of man's purity of heart and spirit. Therefore listen to your inner voice, and go by your conscience. Have no illusions about yourself. Accept yourself the way you are. Only then will you be able to accord other people their due respect.

Learning

Learning is a continuous process. From the beginning of his life to the end, man is learning. As children we learn from our parents and as adults from our peers. As students we learn from our teachers, and as teachers, we learn from our students. Experience teaches us many things. Self-education through books, lectures and seminars is another mode of acquiring knowledge.

Learning leaves an indelible imprint in our life. Parents inculcate in us virtues, which remain with us till we breathe our last. Friends influence the way we behave. Teachers help shape our future.

Experience aids our progress and lectures inspire us to explore new horizons.

Consciously or otherwise we keep learning throughout our life. Hence we should only imbibe good and valuable lessons. Wrong knowledge can ruin our future and our life.

Seek and You Shall Find

Finding answers to questions is not a mechanical act. It gives rise to new possibilities and makes one look for fresh avenues. There is an old story in the Mahabharata. Once, the Pandavas reached a lake to quench their thirst. There they encountered a celestial spirit, which refused them water till they had satiated its curiosity. It asked them several questions.

> *Man has made path-breaking discoveries every time he has tried to find answers to questions that have troubled his mind.*

The Pandavas could not provide satisfactory answers and turned to stone. But Yudhisthira, the eldest of the Pandavas, emerged triumphant. He held his own with his scintillating repartee and brought his brothers back to life.

In today's context, the story might seem far-fetched. But it vividly brings out the importance of the quest for knowledge. Man has made path-breaking discoveries every time he has tried to find answers to questions that have troubled his mind. And he has always made new beginnings!

Moral issues

It is a fact that the present age symbolises growth and development. It promises endless possibilities. But that it is riddled with problems and difficulties is also a fact. Far greater than the social, financial and political problems are the moral issues.

> *It is possible to live without success, as long as your integrity is maintained. But without character, success is meaningless.*

Unfortunately, while we have made rapid strides in science and technology, we have lost touch with our moral values. Everyday we are moving further from the truth. We have lost our strength of character somewhere along the way. It is a sad commentary on life that on the road to success, we had to leave behind our values. We have to ensure that they remain a vital part of our lives. For it is possible to live without success, as long as your integrity is maintained. But without character, success is meaningless.

Word Power

Baan means an arrow and *vaani* means speech. Both the words are similar not only in letter but also in spirit. Like a properly aimed arrow is bound to hit its target, similarly, the use of right speech helps one attain his goal. But there is a difference. The after-effect of words is far more devastating. You can take out a poisonous arrow that pierces your body. But it is not possible to nullify the effects of a thoughtless utterance.

> **Good emotions give rise to good words. We need to cherish such words.**

An arrow only wounds the body but our language is capable of hurting the mind. It conveys emotions. Good emotions give rise to good words. We need to cherish such words.

That is why Kabir Das has written:

> *You cannot compare wealth and words, learned men discern*
> *Even diamonds can be paid for, but not brilliant words.*

Time is the Best Healer

Time is the most powerful force. No one has been able to challenge time to date, and no one ever will. There is a time and place for every thing. Things move at their own pace. Every day, the sun rises and sets at a fixed time. Trees, flowers and leaves grow and die in a pre-determined cycle. The rules of time are universal. They cannot be challenged.

A human being is a part of the cosmos. He too must move with time. Even time follows its cycle. Unravel this mystery called time and you can control it. For what can be done today, was not possible yesterday. And what can be done today should not be left for tomorrow.

Zero

Zero does not have an identity of its own. But when it combines with any other number, it enhances the latter's significance.

If zero is the beginning, it is also the end. If it means gain, it also implies loss. Zero has the power to convert the finite into infinite and the eternal into the ephemeral. When 'one' combines with 'zero' it becomes ten. A zero added to ten makes one hundred; one hundred become one thousand; a thousand, a lakh and this goes on till infinity...!

Unity

There is a very famous story of a man who called his sons and gave each of them a thin thread, and asked them to break it. They snapped it at the very first try. Next, he took many threads, bunched them together and asked his sons to attempt the same feat again. This time the thin threads had combined to become one, hence they could not break it.

> *History has documented several stories of how unity among people has helped achieve great victories.*

The story holds a message: The importance of unity. Differences, divisions, partitions only weaken us. History has documented several stories of how unity among people has helped achieve great victories. A blade of grass has no identity. But many blades of grass combine to form a rope. And the very same rope can firmly check even a rogue elephant!

Fear

It is a rule of nature that if you fear something, you will definitely find it coming your way. If we are scared of disappointments, sure enough we will experience disappointment in life. If we are scared of darkness, we will soon find ourselves being engulfed by it. Actually, fear does not have any power whatsoever, of its own. It is we who give it undue importance. Fear is our inability to act as we would like to. We feel scared when we accept defeat in totality – with our mind, body and soul. Sometimes we must gauge the strengths that lie within us. We will be surprised to find that our strengths far surpass our weaknesses.

> *If you fear something, you will definitely find it coming your way.*

Rhythm

Everything in nature has a rhythm of its own. We breathe in a rhythmic fashion, our heartbeats have a rhythm of their own. The air moves with its own force and the water flows with a different rhythm. The rustling of leaves, rumbling of thunder and a flash of lightning, each has its own rhythm. The sun and moon rise and set in their cycles. Day rhythmically follows night.

> *We should be grateful to this harmony in nature that ensures the smooth flow of life. When life moves on in this fashion, our progress becomes easy.*

Nature has passed on to us this harmony. This harmony is the result of love and a sense of belonging that ties us to one another. We should be grateful to this harmony in nature that ensures the smooth flow of life. When life moves on in this fashion, our progress becomes easy.

Holy Pilgrimage

 80

When a person undertakes a pilgrimage, he is absolved of all his problems, and it also gives a new direction to his life. Ancient philosophies and teachings have been described as a form of pilgrimage. Their treatises help dispel the darkness of ignorance.

Sages and teachers have also been worshipped in India. They impart learning and knowledge to their students.

But the most holy of all these is the purity of our inner conscience and our strength of mind. Coupled with our self-confidence, these qualities help us in life's pilgrimage and enable us to taste success.

Battles are Won and Lost in the Mind

81

Kabir has said that all battles are won and lost in the mind. The meaning is very clear. If pessimism clouds your mind, it will engulf your life with disappointment. Let enthusiasm and happiness spring from your mind. It is the state of mind that determines what your life is going to be like.

> **If we do not exploit the hidden strengths of our mind,**
> **then they are of no use to us.**

The battles of our life are not fought and won on the basis of our physical strength but on the basis of our mind. Harivanshrai Bachchan says:

Within man
There are many things that are excellent
Life gives you an opportunity
To exploit it.
And that man is happy
Who succeeds in his effort to do this.

If we do not exploit the hidden strengths of our mind, then they are of no use to us. Anyone can pick up an unlit stick but no one will dare pick up a flaming torch!

True Goals

What is the secret behind man's progress? Man once survived by creating fire from stone. How did he come such a long way? The secret behind his development was his ability to ask questions. In search of answers man was able to progress this far.

> *Those who dare to ask and find answers to many questions become successful in their lives.*

What is this world? Who is its creator? How and why do things happen? Answers to these questions have helped human beings progress. Our life would still be a question mark if these questions had not been raised and answered. That is why it is said, 'Seek and you'll get the answer!' Those who dare to ask and find answers to many questions become successful in their lives. And questions raised by life provide their own goals. And once the goal is fixed then success automatically follows.

Determination

There are times in our lives when we feel more despair than hope. We experience circumstances where we feel that our difficulties loom larger than our benefits. We find it difficult to carry the weight of our burden. But this does not mean that we should lose confidence in our capabilities.

> *It is not a crime to fall, but it is a crime not to recover after the fall!*

The sun does not stop shining even if it is covered with thick clouds. Can the dark clouds take away the light it covers? Why should we then lose faith in ourselves? The waning moon soon returns in its original form and shape, a broken tree sprouts new branches and life. It is not a crime to fall, but it would be one if we did not recover after the fall!

Ability and Endeavour

Just as a small lamp dispels the enveloping darkness, a tiny piece of rope can tether the mighty elephant. A hammer can break many a boulder into tiny pieces. But is the lamp larger than the darkness it illuminates? Is a rope equal to the elephant? Can the hammer ever be bigger than the boulders it breaks? The answer is no, for all these things are very small. But their inherent qualities are so strong that their size really does not matter. The smallest ability and endeavour can triumph over the biggest of difficulties

> *Human ingenuity can triumph over the biggest of difficulties.*

This is the basis of our capabilities. Human ingenuity can triumph over the biggest of difficulties. Just a few years of our education make us so strong and capable that we can guide our lives in the desired direction. With a few years of hard work and dedication we ensure a lifetime of happiness!

Worldly Wise

God has created beautiful things in this world. They are more interesting than any story, more mysterious than any novel. They are also more lyrical than any song and more musical than any tune. If the treatises are endless, then knowledge too is unlimited. The world is infinite, but our life is finite.

Soul Curry for you and me

Our limited existence on this earth can be made happy when we learn not only to appreciate the wondrous things on earth, but also stay clear of all the hindrances, wickedness and false illusions that exist around us. In the ocean of the universe, our life is like the boat that floats on the ocean. The boat stays in the water, but see that no water gets into the boat!

Flow

As long as the flow of water is thin and weak, it cautiously navigates the obstacles that come its way. But, as its flow starts to gain speed and strength, it starts destroying those very obstacles that had come in its way. Water with its strength decides its own course and direction.

> *Difficulties are in direct proportion to our inner strength. If we are weak our difficulties get blown out of proportion.*

We should also navigate our course of life like the flow of water. We should not hesitate in removing and throwing away obstacles that hamper our progress. Difficulties are in direct proportion to our inner strength. If we are weak inside, our difficulties get blown out of proportion. But if we remain strong and determined we can overcome our obstacles easily. There is an old adage that says that a man may fear the storm and not sail his boat in the sea. But sitting on the shore will not protect him from the storm.

Doubts

There is a proverb that says that words like 'if 'and 'but' spoil our world. We use these words only when we are in doubt.

> *Doubts make us stray from the right path. In our weakened state of mind, it will not take us long to confuse a rope for a snake.*

Doubts do not appear in isolation. Weakness, hesitation, ignorance and confusion accompany them. These qualities weaken our mental strength and render it useless. Doubts make us stray from the right path. In our weakened state of mind, it will not take us long to confuse a rope for a snake.

Hence, in order to progress in life it is first necessary to eliminate all the doubts we have from our minds. For this you need strong determination and the ability to take firm decisions.

Experience, the Best Teacher

Our life is a collection of experiences and incidents. The good and bad, sweet and the sour experiences are our teachers. They provide valuable guidance and serve as our true well-wishers.

> *Experiences gleaned from life are far more important, relevant and significant than the lessons learnt from books.*

Experiences gleaned from life are far more important, relevant and significant than the lessons learnt from books. These experiences turn our life into a book, a valuable lesson that becomes a guiding light for others to follow.

Pace

Today, the whole world is in a constant hurry. Every one is trying to race and outpace the other. This only goes to prove the fact that speed has become extremely important in our lives. Everyone attains his goal sooner or later. But in today's world, he is the greatest who reaches his goal first.

With this burden and tension in our minds, we are all running the race of life. To win we do not need ordinary but extraordinary inner resources!

Act Now!

Debate has always taken place about what is more important: destiny or action. The great politician-philosopher Chanakya had this to say in a simple and straightforward manner about the issue: *No matter what is written in your destiny, it is not possible to achieve it without taking action.* If you are destined to eat mangoes and lie down below a mango tree, the fruit will not automatically fall into your mouth. You will have to pluck them from the tree!

> *You cannot deny that fate is powerful. But when faced with action, destiny is forced to concede defeat.*

His remark was made centuries ago, but it is relevant even today. It is very true that destiny does not favour those who lie in wait for things to happen to them. You cannot deny that fate is powerful. But when faced with action, destiny is forced to concede defeat.

Beautiful Things — Words

God created this world. He made human beings, the sun, moon and stars, rivers, mountains and valleys. He also created birds and

animals. He made the world extremely beautiful. But He made something far more wonderful than all these – words. Nothing is more beautiful or creative than words. Words are not merely attractive, they are powerful too. Words have the power of changing others and thereby influencing not only man, but society and the country as well. Only the right interpretation will enable us to derive the right meaning of the words. Deriving inspiration and enthusiasm from a few words will help us become better human beings.

Memories and imagination

Memories dwell on time gone by and imagination speculates about the future. Both these states exist only in the mind and have no connection with our present.

And they are responsible for giving a new perspective to our lives. If our memories inspire us, it is our dreams and imagination that instill us with strength and courage. We can stabilise our present by taking a leaf from the past and by taking a look at what our future has in store for us. We must take full advantage of this because opportunities do not come time and again.

The Test

In the race of life, man lives with a definite purpose. He strives to fulfil his purpose. But whilst doing so he encounters difficulties, problems and countless obstacles.

We call them problems or difficulties. But in truth these are tests of our innermost desires. Until we pass through the test of fire, we will lag behind and will not be able to reach our final goal.

Magnification

Learning or knowledge is like a microscope. It helps us realise qualities that are hidden in our personalities.

A microscope is an instrument that enables us to see even the smallest of things. This does not show us anything new, it merely magnifies those qualities which are already present in the object.

Learning or knowledge is like a microscope. It helps us realise the qualities that are hidden in our personalities. Quite often we are unaware of these qualities. Knowledge and learning not only make us capable but also help in developing our personality. When our personality is complete it becomes very easy for us to achieve success.

Belief and Knowledge

To believe and to know – we rely a great deal on the experiences that these two words indicate. When we are not able to understand something, we begin to believe it. But often, blind belief is not enough.

Until and unless we try to discover or desire to know more about a thing, we will remain miles away from the truth. Only knowledge can reveal the truth. It is very easy to believe a lie. As far as the truth is concerned, it will always out.

Misgivings

All of us fear opposition, difficulties and failure. Hence, even the most confident person is often startled by his own shadow. We are worried that we will fail, forgetting that the seeds of success lie within us. We

are scared of falling ill. What we do not realise is that we invite diseases by neglecting our own health. We fear that we will lose our wealth, ignoring the fact that our capabilities are far greater than any external trappings.

Our fears do not arise from any external force. They lie within us, in the form of our doubts. We let our weaknesses overshadow our strengths, in turn letting fear get the better of us.

> *Our fears do not arise from any external force. They lie within us, in the form of our doubts.*

We should assess our capabilities well. Only then will we be rid of our fears and doubts and will be able to lead our lives in an effective and progressive manner.

Our intelligence is Supreme

Most of us have read the *Panchatantra* fable of the small rabbit and the ferocious lion. Every day the lion would devour one animal from the jungle. This went on till the tiny rabbit outwitted him. He showed the lion his reflection in a well, saying that this was another king of the jungle. The lion foolishly attacked it and was drowned. The story is a simple one but its moral is significant.

> *Intelligence is man's greatest strength. Where weapons and might fail, intelligence reigns supreme*

Intelligence is man's greatest strength. Where weapons and might fail, intelligence reigns supreme. Your intelligence will never let you down, it will never fail you. Without intelligence we are like a lifeless statue. It is our mind that helps us achieve whatever we aspire to.

Measure of Success

You must not judge a successful man by the social status or position he enjoys today. Rather, the success of a man must be measured by the amount of difficulties he has faced in achieving his success and by the obstacles he has surmounted. It is a fallacy that a successful man faces less problems than the individual who has failed. The difference between the two lies in the fact that a man who is successful makes light of all his difficulties and problems.

> *It is a fallacy that a successful man faces less problems than the individual who has failed. A man who is successful makes light of all his difficulties and problems.*

We should be grateful that hurdles come our way. Not only do they make us stronger but they also give us the strength to face other difficulties that lie in store for us.

Soundness of Body and Mind

A healthy mind resides in a healthy body. Though it sounds trite, it is extremely relevant to all of us. If your body is healthy your mind will remain sound and only then will you be able to chart the course of your life well. This in turn can lead to success.

To lead a fruitful life you need a sound mind and healthy body. To a certain extent you also need wealth. And ultimately it is up to you to ensure that you stay fit and fine, both mentally and physically.

Small Things

100

We often do not give any importance to the small things in life and tend to ignore them. But what we forget is that any big achievement is carved out of a small beginning. The mighty oak grows from a tiny acorn. Similarly, tiny words meet to make a learned tome. Each heart-beat contributes its mite in keeping you alive. And centuries are made only after adding one day to another!

> *Any big achievement is carved out of a small beginning.*
> *If you ignore the small things in life, you will not be*
> *able to achieve any kind of success.*

To understand the importance of small things you must take a look at a scientist's work. A scientist examines tiny, often unimportant events and goes on to make great discoveries. If you ignore the seemingly small things in life, you will not be able to achieve any kind of success. After all, little drops of water, little grains of sand, make the mighty ocean and the present land.

Discovering the World

101

We hardly know anything about the world we live in and we do not try hard enough to know it. Our planet is far more interesting than any story that you might have heard. It is more attractive than any poem, sweeter than any music and more mysterious than any novel. We confuse our immediate environment with the world. We do not realise that it is far greater than what our imagination can conceive!

Knowledge means discovering the world around you and learning more about it. You cannot explore the world through books. Be awake, be alert to things around you and you will be able to learn much more about the world. He who has learnt the most about the world can win it over!

No Age Bar

It is true that greatness comes with age, but then this is not the only criterion for assessing it. Knowledge, experience, ability and cleverness that often accompany age also determine the greatness of a person. And if an individual achieves tremendous success at a relatively young age, he will be counted amongst the great ones.

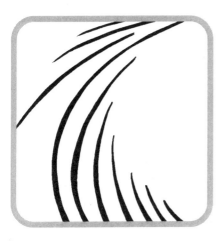

Abilities are not linked to age. They are related to intelligence.

Abilities are not linked to age. They are related to intelligence. Genius and intelligence cannot be counted in years. They are timeless and universal.

Curiosity

Take a look at history. If we try to unfold what is behind the major achievements of the past, it will probably be our curiosity. Small, perhaps insignificant events first provoke curiosity. His enthusiasm to know more and more led man to revolutionary discoveries. These new developments culminated in the contemporary age. Unless we try to satisfy our curiosity we will never be able to attain further knowledge and learning.

> *Unless we try to satisfy our curiosity we will never be able to attain further knowledge and learning.*

It is a fact that curiosity coupled with enthusiasm gives rise to our desires. We work hard to fulfil our desires. Our efforts and hard work will help us achieve our goal.

Successful Life

104

Most of us think that a man is successful because he has fame or money. But this is not necessarily true. The life of every individual is invaluable if he has lived in the right manner.

It is a fact that nothing is more important than life itself. We can mould and shape our lives in whichever way we want to. But our bad qualities can completely sour our entire existence. If you lead your life diligently, with determination and hard work, you can make a huge success of it. Infact you can turn it into a paradise on earth!

Journey

105

Before setting out on a journey, we should be sure of our destination and goals. We must assess whether we can complete the journey we have undertaken and whether we will be able to face the difficulties that come our way. If we do not plan things before we set forth, we are likely to either end up nowhere or reach the wrong destination.

We should avoid making mistakes. We are mere mortals, our strengths are limited and the time that we have is very little. Hence

we should tread with careful deliberation and thought. Only then will we be able to reach our destination.

Yes or No?

Do you remember the times you say 'yes' and 'no'? Believe it or not the usage of these two words reflects our personality.

'Yes' is a reflection of our confidence, our desires and our beliefs. 'No' mirrors our defeatist nature. These two words appear simple but if they are not used properly or in the correct manner they can change your thinking and personality as well.

> *If you agree to do something wrong it is a sure sign of your weakness but being able to say no shows that your character is firm and strong!*

If you agree to do something wrong it is a sure sign of your weakness but being able to say no shows that your character is firm and strong! It also shows that you will not be easily influenced by whatever comes your way.

Uncertainty

When Alexander the Great was asked the secret of his success he replied that when he set his mind on something, he never turned his back on it. His reply applies not only to his own life, but to all our lives as well.

Uncertainty renders impotent the mental and physical capabilities of any person. But if your decisions are firm, then you can surmount any problem.

Step by Step

A small lamp cannot dispel all the darkness in the world. But it can definitely illuminate our immediate surroundings. This light enables us to take a few steps forward. And as we move ahead, we realise that the light is automatically showing us the way onwards. In this way it is possible to conquer the world. Our knowledge is similar to this light. We cannot completely eradicate ignorance. But with the little wisdom that we gain we are able to see our own way more clearly.

Every man has adequate understanding, intelligence and knowledge so that he can slowly, step by step, reach his goal. But in order to do so, every individual must realise the potential and scope of his wisdom.

intelligence is Supreme

Man is the greatest of all living things in the universe because of the intelligence he possesses and his ability to reason.

> *A healthy mind must cultivate new thoughts and discipline. We can develop our minds only by learning.*

Man's mental prowess implies that he can apply his reasoning to work towards a better future. This ensures that he progresses in life. But for this he must think in the right direction. A healthy mind must cultivate new thoughts and discipline. We can develop our minds only by learning. And as our minds grow from strength to strength, we can make our dreams come true.

investment in Knowledge

There is nothing in the world that will always remain profitable... Every venture faces the risk of losses. And, there is no business – investment that shows only profits. Yet, there is one investment in life that will never incur a loss. You need not be scared of losing it or it passing into oblivion. And that is investment in knowledge.

> *Knowledge is like a well that will never dry up.*

Knowledge is like a well that will never dry up. It not only gives us wealth but also helps us to achieve success, self-confidence and self-reliance!

Proper Use of Time

111

It is true that life never waits for anyone and leaves no footprints
behind. A moment lost is lost forever. Once it is gone it is impossible
to recall the past. Yet, if man wants he can conquer time by
using it wisely to attain strength, greatness and desirable
qualities. Using it well means that we do not waste or underutilise it.
If we use time properly then it will always stay with us in the form of
our qualities and capabilities.

The man who fully exploits the time and opportunity given to him
will be a complete man, a man who will be at peace with himself.

Find a Purpose

112

Men often seek a variety of goals – knowledge, wealth, strength,
fame and glory. They have huge ambitions and dreams and labour
hard to realise their hopes. And their ultimate goal is success.

*A life without a definite goal has no meaning. People
who live a meaningless existence are not only unhappy
themselves but in turn make others unhappy too.*

A life without a definite goal has no meaning and this aimless life cannot inspire anyone. People who live a meaningless existence are not only unhappy themselves but in turn make others unhappy too.

Every successful individual has a fixed target in his life. With determination, he must concentrate on achieving this very target. His goal is the driving force behind all his actions.

The Really Fortunate

Some people are born fortunate, or are called destiny's children. But you cannot live your life waiting for things to happen. The concept of destiny and misfortune are the creations of people who lack the confidence in their ability to achieve their goals. People who wait for destiny to favour them and change their course of life will always be unsuccessful in life. An individual's success is not dependent on his fate. Rather, it is the result of his hard work.

People who are willing to take risks, who are capable and believe in action are the really fortunate ones.

Self-dependence

In our everyday lives we often seek help from others. But we cannot always look to others for succour. Even medicine loses its potency if it is taken over a long period of time. Similarly, life has no meaning if you continuously look to others for help.

> *If there is anything you must depend on then it is your own capabilitiy, mental strength and inner confidence.*

If there is anything you must depend on then it is your own capabilitiy, mental strength and confidence. This will make you self-dependent. The doors of success will always beckon the self-reliant.

Children

We look upon children as an incarnation of God for they are free of all evil. Childhood is like clay, which can be moulded into any shape. Values and lessons that are imbibed in our childhood stay with us forever. I fervently wish that every child in our country be given the opportunity to grow and be able to tap his potential fully. Who knows...a child who seems ordinary today might well be the genius of the future!

Concentration
116

In life, the road to success is reached through knowledge. And we can gain true knowledge through concentration. Concentration is the key that helps us unlock the doors of knowledge. And the success of any venture depends on the concentrated effort behind it.

Complete dedication and concentration can make even the impossible possible. That is the secret of success. It is concentration that enables us to grasp victory even in the face of defeat.

Self-Confidence

All of us have confidence in ourselves, in our ability and capabilities. But what is more important is that others have the same confidence in you. Self-confidence is essential in life. But it is equally important to win the faith and confidence of others.

When the smile on a person's face reflects his confidence, it carves out a path for a promising future. His actions reflect his greatness. People will never hesitate to follow his orders. He is, in the truest sense, a leader of the people.

intelligent Man

A bird does not fear the skies, a tiger is not scared of the jungle and a fish is completely at home in water. Similarly an educated and intelligent man is not overawed by difficulties. He faces them with calmness and fortitude.

> *Education not only endows you with learning but also makes you fearless and brave.*

Education not only endows you with learning but also makes you fearless and brave. And an intelligent person is able to bring even the most difficult of circumstances under his control.

True Dedication

If you aspire to an ideal life you will need knowledge, learning, art, strength and wealth. But it is not easy to acquire all these qualities. What you need is hard work and dedication. With dedication, your actions will bear fruit.

If you have full faith in your ability to work hard, then you will definitely reap the results of your hard work.

Time and Opportunities

120

Time is man's greatest teacher. But time waits for no man. You can be successful in life if you learn to utilise time in the right manner. Do not postpone things if you can do them today. Learn what you can today, for the present minute is in your power. Time, once gone, cannot be recalled, and nobody knows what the future has in store for us.

> *Learn what you can today, for the present minute is in your power.*

Man's greatest achievments result from his exploiting the present in the best possible way. Ensure that you live every moment of your present life to its fullest, your tomorrow will automatically be insured. Hence, it is said that life, time and opportunities come only once!

infotainment

Modern life gives equal importance to learning and entertainment. No wonder the radio, television and the computer
are considered not just means of entertainment, but sources of learning as well.

The combination of these two distinct streams of information and entertainment, has given rise to a completely new concept.
This new discipline is called infotainment –which is information plus entertainment.

Unlimited Wealth

An individual's unlimited wealth is his knowledge. No one can steal it or destroy it. It is a limitless treasure trove – the more you expend it, the more it grows.

> *The spring of knowledge sustains you in your moments of difficulties.*

There comes a time when your luck runs out. Your actions do not get the desired results. The spring of knowledge sustains you in your moments of difficulties. It is that evergreen source that continuously helps you attain the success, respect and wealth that you seek.

inspiring Dreams

Everyone dreams. Our dreams embody our innermost desires. They reflect the great heights to which our ambitions can soar. But dreams do not turn into reality overnight. You have to work hard to realise them. The day you are able to convert your dreams into reality you have definitely achieved something in life. When we dream, we are filled with hope and we seldom despair.

> *Dreams are the stuff that life is made of. They provide us with inspiration.*

Dreams are the stuff that life is made of. They provide us with inspiration. An individual who has the ability to translate his dreams into reality and fulfil his ambitions is a great man.

Mistakes

Who does not make mistakes? No one is perfect and to err is human. Even the man who comes close to perfection will err sometime. And a man who never commits mistakes achieves nothing. A complete man learns from the mistakes he has made and does not repeat them. Just as a diamond sparkles only after it is repeatedly rubbed against stone, a man does not become complete unless he has made a few mistakes. The road to success is paved with mistakes.

You must accept your mistakes and in turn learn from them. Only then can you move ahead and savour success. To do this one requires

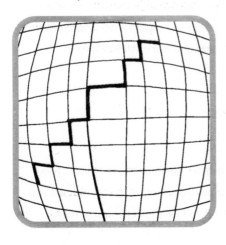

a degree of strength, courage and ability, and success awaits those who put their mistakes behind them and move ahead with their lives.

Have Faith in Yourself

Have you ever tried to understand yourself, tap your potential and realise your ambitions? Do you have confidence in yourself? If the answer is 'no', it is time for self-assessment. You will discover that you possess the same qualities that you have always admired in others. All of us have infinite potential. We only need to discover it.

Those who have faith in themselves, identify and trust their own potential and inner capabilities, will never face failure. Self-confidence leads to success.

> *All of us have infinite potential. We only need to discover it.*

Power of the Pen

126

From the dawn of civilisation, man has made many discoveries. Indubitably, books are the greatest of them all. The concept of a modern era would have been unimaginable without the wealth of words. Absence of books would have silenced scriptures and handicapped progress. History would have gone undocumented. The future would be bleak indeed. Books have served mankind as a vehicle of progress through generations. This legacy will help future generations build a better tomorrow.

Hence, the importance of the written word is undisputable. They are the springs of knowledge. Wisdom stored in books can help us turn the world of our imagination into reality.

Just Dues

127

When does a man have a spark in his eyes, a bounce in his stride?
When does his face light up with a thousand delighted smiles? Or
when does he find his world turning rosy? Obviously, it is when
people congratulate him on his accomplishments. Or when they
appreciate his abilities and accept his superiority. It is a feeling of
justified pride, which makes the world appear different to him.

The Gifted

128

Nature's bounty is unlimited. Here every atom has its own distinct
use. Every alphabet is used to make words. Every musical note gives
rise to sweet music.

Every tree has its own shade. And every individual is capable in his
own unique way. It is not necessary to search for virtues elsewhere.
Look inwards, and you will find them within you.

It is essential to recognise and exploit your inner potential and put
it to good use.

> *It is not necessary to search for virtues elsewhere. Look*
> *inwards, and you will find them within you.*

Recognise this truth, experience and apply it to your life, you will
scale great heights.

Truth and Non-violence

129

Truth, non-violence, peace and love – these are much used words
that have been passed from one generation to another. But
it took one man to prove that these are just not empty words but

powerful weapons in the hands of mankind. Mahatma Gandhi, the father of our nation, proved to the whole world that the biggest of wars could be won on the strength of truth and non-violence!

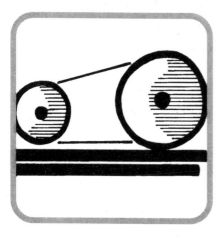

Common Sense

You do not need to read great works of literature or have wise teachers to acquire common sense. Knowledge is being aware of the facts of life. It comes out of experience and looking at things in a different perspective. It is a product of a new thought process and a new awakening. You need to find answers to your questions yourself. You have to be in tune with the times and absorb all the knowledge you can. Events of today fast become the history of tomorrow.

> *You need to find answers to your questions yourself. You have to be in tune with the times and absorb all the knowledge you can.*

The classic five 'W's and one 'H'– When? Why? Where? What? And How? – help us to develop common sense.

Opportunity

Opportunity knocks at your door only once. And when it does, it does so unexpectedly. Every individual however, gets the right chance at least once in his lifetime. Those who exploit every opportunity that comes their way are the ones who succeed in life.

Effort will bear fruit only if it is timely. You must strike while the iron is hot. Grab the opportunity with both hands for you only get it once!

Every Difficulty Brings its Own Lesson

Learning is a continuous process. You keep learning irrespective of age, subject or means. Every dawn brings with it a new lesson. Each problem teaches us something new. Every cloud has a silver lining. You learn from your past mistakes and ensure a better future.

> *Every dawn brings with it a new lesson. Each problem teaches us something new.*

Hence it is said, stagnation sets in the moment you stop learning. It stunts growth. Only those who strive to acquire new knowledge progress in life.

Truly Brave

Sometimes your life takes an unexpected turn due to circumstances. But brave are those who change the course of events. They are the masters of their own destiny. Time is all encompassing. It is elusive. Courageous are those who grab it with open hands. A storm spells destruction. Courageous are those who weather adversities confidently and even change the course of events.

This is not only bookish knowledge but a fact of life. With courage and conviction, a man can overcome any difficulty with a smile.

Knowledge is Strength

A man can rule over the universe but cannot conquer knowledge. Knowledge has no boundaries. Knowledge helps to document the glorious history of the world and provides a glimpse of the future. Knowledge helps man to unravel the mysteries of the earth. Information trapped in medical books is indeed a panacea. It helps man to save his fellow beings from the jaws of death.

When used wisely, knowledge promotes progress. It is the most powerful tool. And man is considered supreme because it is he who possesses this tool!

Wisdom

Don't all of us work hard? All of us put in our best efforts. It is hard work that keeps our life moving. But if your efforts are combined with a bit of planning, it will help you to live a happy and peaceful life. Use your abilities to the fullest. All your dreams will slowly but surely come true.

Endless Possibilities

A seed is small in size. But it carries in its womb leaves, flowers, fruits, nay even the whole tree. The human brain is very much like a seed. It may not have a great shape and size. But it traps within itself endless possibilities. It is a fountainhead of thoughts and promises that can be fulfilled.

> *We need to discover ourselves, and understand our motives.*

We need to discover ourselves, and understand our motives. Once we realise our full potential, we will be able to do precisely what we want to do in our lives.

Of Money and Wealth

Money is important. But it is not the most important thing in life. Agreed, from time immemorial money has always given man security and comfort. Intelligence is the most powerful tool that a man possesses. Yet you cannot overlook the importance of wealth. Money may not be everything. But one needs money to lead a decent life.

> *Intelligence is the most powerful tool that a man possesses. Yet you cannot overlook the importance of wealth.*

Money does not grow on any tree. Nor is it possible to produce it. You can only earn money. And you can do this either by using your intelligence or through sheer hard work.

Soul Curry
for you and me

Flights of Fancy

138

We cannot reach out to the sun. But there is nothing wrong in desiring to do so. We cannot pluck stars from the sky, but there is no harm in dreaming about it. Thinking big not only helps the mind to grow, but also inspires you to perform truly great deeds. Do not curtail your imagination. Let your thoughts take wing.

Wisdom or Wealth?

139

There is an old saying that it is better to have an empty purse than an empty mind. This is absolutely true. For empty coffers can always be replenished by a clever person. Only enlightenment dispels darkness of ignorance. It illuminates a vacant mind.

It is not only the right but also the duty of every citizen to drive away ignorance from his country, society, his house and most important, his mind. It is knowledge that has the power to satiate your innermost desires. Sagacity brings with it strength, well-being and prosperity.

Laughter is Wealth

In this world no man is so wealthy that he can live without laughter and smiles, and no man so poor that he does not have the wealth of laughter and smiles. A smile is a treasure trove, which bestows untold riches upon the person who receives it, yet the person who parts with it will never be impoverished. Laughter and smiles break out for a minute, yet their memory remains undimmed throughout one's life.

Fixed Target

If you have a set goal in mind even the smallest of efforts will bear fruit. History documents countless examples of small actions, which have led to big results. To climb the highest mountain peaks you have to start at the base! If you have a definite purpose you do not wait for opportunities to knock at your door. In fact you change the course of your own destiny.

Instead of wasting his time in mundane matters, if a man moves ahead single-mindedly on his chosen path, success is sure to follow him.

I remember a few lines from Harivanshrai Bachchan's *Madhushaala*:

*A man who wants to drink leaves home in search of
a liquor den,
He is confused as to which road he should choose,
Different people guide him down different lanes, but
I advise him
Choose one path, stick to it and you will automatically find
what you are looking for.*

Love Means Surrender

If anyone asks me to define an ideal couple in simple and straight forward terms, I would say: 'If one partner says something, the other one agrees. And the saints call them both wise!'

> *You can call two people a couple only when the two are combined to form one 'we'. When we shed our ego what remains behind is the 'us' factor.*

You can call two people a couple only when the two are combined to form one 'we'. When we shed our ego what remains behind is the 'us' factor — a sense of belonging, a team spirit. This union leaves no

room for egos – what remains is love, affection, respect and belonging, for and towards each other.

What the union needs is one small step that is filled with self-confidence and love. The day you surrender your ego, you will discover that the other person's ego too will disappear. It cannot sustain itself. I am very confident about this!

Family

143

What is a family? A family is an amalgamation of relationships bonded together by love. This institution is created and sustained by duty, selflessness and discipline.

A family means a union where the members stay together in times of laughter and tears, happiness and sorrow.

Hankering for One's Roots

144

As man started discovering new places, the world began to shrink in size. Progress crossed boundaries and seeped into every lane, town and country. And man even reached the moon
in his quest of these possibilities.

> *A man may become famous, earn a lot of wealth and status but he will find peace of mind and happiness only in his own homeland and with his own people.*

But no matter where man may make his home, he will always miss his roots, his soil, his people and his country. He is constantly searching for the sweet smell of his soil, the ink of the letters from home, the warmth and the affection of his own people. He may become famous, earn a lot of wealth and status but he will find peace of mind and happiness only in his own homeland and with his own people.

That is why his heart and mind seek opportunities to constantly connect and stay in touch with his roots.

The importance of Nature

I recently noticed that an old tree that had stood for years in a lane, had fallen in the middle of the road. It was a huge, evergreen tree. Its branches had provided the lane with immense shade. Sifting through its leaves, the warm breeze acquired a welcome coolness. Some vendors had set up a shop at its base that had become the source of their livelihood. Children used to play below the huge shade of the tree. The tree had provided shelter and support to many people.

But now the tree has fallen and the lane is scorched by harsh sunlight. It is as if the lane lies exposed to the whole world. The pleasant cool breeze has given way to hot air. Birds that had earlier nested amidst its branches, are now seeking other trees. The children have mysteriously vanished. Now, one can only see destitution and empty space throughout the day.

> *If trees and plants are not essential, why would nature create them? We are not felling trees, we are aiming the axe directly at our feet.*

Imagine the felling of one tree can have such a monumental effect on its surroundings and disrupt so many lives. And yet, every day, people are felling and destroying trees for their own selfish purpose. Man is killing nature. He is denuding countless forests. Soon the whole earth will look like the lane where the tree once stood. Man wants to seek other planets to live on but has no qualms in destroying life on the very planet he lives in.

If trees and plants are not essential, why would nature create them? We are not felling trees, we are aiming the axe directly at our feet.

It is true that only God is the creator. We will not become gods giving life to one tree, but we will definitely become good and conscientious citizens of our country.

What Our Fingers Say

146

It is a fact that no man in the world is complete in himself. There is something lacking in each one of us. Yet, the eternal truth is that there is no individual who does not have at least a few good qualities in him.

The Game of Life

In the game of life, we experience the joy of winning and the sorrow of losing. At times things happen quickly, at other times they get delayed. In life we will meet with disappointments, at times, success. We seek help from the ones who are close to us but we also trust people who are not so close to us. On one hand you are full of doubt, on the other you radiate self-confidence.

> *Life is full of reality and illusions. There is a sense of belonging as well as a sense of detachment. There is freedom but it comes with discipline.*

Life is full of reality and illusions. There is a sense of belonging as well as a sense of detachment. There is freedom but it comes with discipline. There is knowledge and science. There is honour and respect. There is wealth, intelligence, the desire to achieve a goal, enthusiasm, etc. All these qualities constitute our life.

Time

No one can escape the strong and all pervading effect of time. Even the sun and the moon get embroiled in time and are shadowed by the eclipse. Disaster strikes silently and stealthily and takes from us our smiles, our happiness, our very lives.

We must face adversity with courage. Troubles, when faced with fortitude diminish, sorrow is reduced, we see a new ray of hope and new avenues open up, putting the smile back on our faces. And that indeed is life!

Disappointment, indecision and darkness – these words are found in the dictionary of those who have not turned its pages and hence have not encountered their opposites. Only the weak are affected by their failures in life. If you know yourself and are aware of your true potential, you will not be disappointed by failure. You will realise that it contains the seeds of your success!

id

150

Id is a festival of happiness and joy. But this happiness does not come easily. To attain it one has to fast for 30 days. Each *roza* is a test or examination in itself. After passing it, one gets a feeling of exhilaration and happiness. This feeling of enthusiasm and happiness is far sweeter than the *sevaiyan*, the special dessert prepared during the Id festival.

We all have a lesson to learn from this festival. In order to attain peace and happiness, one has to work hard, make big sacrifices and have the necessary self-control to resist temptation.

New Year

The freshness of the new year, its new enthusiasm;
  Its wishes, colours and desires are all new;
  Promises and determination are new, with a definition of their own,
  The new year brings a new determination to keep one's resolutions.

> *Unless a man's mind and heart is filled with new desires and ambitions, it is futile to even dream of success.*

Every dawn ushers in a new day. The new year inspires us to ponder over the mixed experiences of the past year. It urges us to resolve to better ourselves in the new year. Unless a man's mind and heart is filled with new desires and ambitions, it is futile to even dream of success. The new year motivates us to move ahead!

Priorities

Every individual has some priorities in his life. A priority is a way of thinking – it is something to be achieved beyond one's capabilities and before schedule. But mere thinking will get you nowhere. To fulfil one's goals and priorities you need grit, determination and hard work.

Simple Questions

Questions are a symbol of man's curiosity and inquiring nature. Whenever a new search, a new curiosity has arisen in man's mind, it has led to a new question. Whenever a new question has arisen in his mind, it has resulted in new possibilities, which in turn have led to a new direction, a new road.

Behind every new invention   lies a simple question. You too should ask questions of yourself, of people around you, of your society. You will realize that only by raising questions will you be able to arrive at the truth; answering questions also leads to the acquisition of knowledge!

> *Behind every new invention lies a simple question. You too should ask questions of yourself, of people around you, of your society.*

Errors and Omissions

154

We often celebrate our success and rue our mistakes. But who does not make mistakes. They say to err is human. A true and honest person learns from his mistakes, errors and omissions. Just as a diamond does not shine until it is rubbed and polished, an individual does not become complete until he meets with a few failures. The road to success is paved with mistakes.

He who realizes his mistakes, learns from them and moves ahead will be the one who will knock at the door of success.

in Step With Progress

155

Since the creation of the universe, man has walked the road to progress. The very same man who created fire from stone, is on the moon now. Progress is continuous. It has its own pace. One who keeps up with this speed, continues to make progress. One who doesn't is left behind. The real meaning of progress is the ability to change oneself to meet the changing demands of time, to stand out in a crowd and to provide for a good life.

Those who are attuned to progress carve out a better future for themselves. A better future creates a better individual.

Keep an open mind – but not so open that you let slip your intelligence through it.

Intelligence is more powerful than a bull – it is a different matter altogether that the bull fetches a greater price in the market place!

> *It is not easy to earn one's bread and butter – you might get your bread easily, but butter is a tougher proposition!*

The road to success is a crooked and bumpy one – One wonders, was this road also created by a government contractor?

If a child asks for a chocolate to do something, then he will definitely become a government employee. Bribe him and get the task completed!

If the child eats the chocolate but refuses to do the work, turns around and causes trouble for you, he is bound to enroll in the police force.

If the child complicates the matter for which he has taken the chocolate, he will become a lawyer.

If a child asks you for a chocolate, grabs money from your pocket and yet delays performing the task, he will definitely become a political leader of the nation.

If the child eats the chocolate in front of you and yet insists that he has not eaten the chocolate, he will definitely become not just a political leader, but a minister as well!

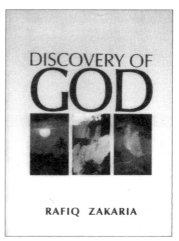

SOME OF OUR BESTSELLERS